The Grand Spring Hunt

Hunting for America's Wild Turkey Gobblers

BART JACOB with **BEN CONGER**

with a new introduction by Lionel Atwill, senior editor,
Field & Stream magazine

THE DERRYDALE PRESS
Lanham and New York

THE DERRYDALE PRESS

Published in the United States of America
by The Derrydale Press
A Member of the Rowman & Littlefield Publishing Group
4720 Boston Way, Lanham, Maryland 20706

Distributed by NATIONAL BOOK NETWORK, INC.

Copyright © 1985, 2002 by Bart Jacob and Ben Conger
New chapter 20, "Uptight Turkeys" copyright © 2002 by Bart Jacob
First Derrydale Printing 2002
ISBN 1-58667-091-3 (pbk. : alk. paper)

The previous edition was cataloged by the Library of Congress as follows:
Jacob, Bart.
　　The grand spring hunt for America's wild turkey gobbler.
　　Includes index.
　　1. Turkey hunting. I. Conger, Ben. II. Title.
SK325.T8J33　　　1985　　　799.2'48619　　　85-6364

♾™ The paper used in this publication meets the minimum requirements of
American National Standard for Information Sciences—Permanence of
Paper for Printed Library Materials, ANSI/NISO Z39.48–1992.
Manufactured in the United States of America.

CONTENTS

PREFACE AND ACKNOWLEDGMENTS

Almost twenty years ago, outdoor writer Ben Conger stopped at the shop and suggested that I write a book about wild turkey hunting.

Many pages of scribble, a chapter at a time, were skillfully entered into Ben's old Kay-Pro word processor by his good wife Pat. After correcting for errors due to misinterpretation of bad spelling and poor writing, the printed pages became a manuscript. Each chapter was reviewed by friends E. Sam Nenno, R. Wayne Bailey and the late Dave Harbour who criticized and corrected the work. Without the editing by Bailey who was a professor of English before becoming Dean Emeritus of Turkey, biologists, and author of the foreword in the original edition of this book, my words would have never seen print.

Now more than fifteen years later the book is to be re-published.

There have been many changes in equipment, guns, bows, cameras, calling devices, etc. In chapter fifteen, for example, most of the equipment has since been replaced by miniaturized video and digital devices. The habits of the wild turkey, however, have stayed pretty much the same. I am thus leaving all of the chapters as originally written.

One new chapter "Uptight Turkeys," based upon my experiences since the first writing, has been added at the end of the book, hopefully for your enjoyment and information.

FOREWORD

The number of wild turkeys and turkey hunters in the United States grows annually. Similarly, harvests of the continent's largest game bird increase. When I was a youth in the hills of southern West Virginia, the only people I could talk with who had actually seen a wild turkey were the oldest grandfathers in the area. In the 1930s I, a stripling, hunted turkeys with my father for several years before seeing one. We desired, in our greed and ignorance, to bag one before they became extinct. Today the bird occupies 49 states—seven more than when Caucasians settled the nation—and the annual harvest may exceed a quarter-million.

I am sometimes asked, "What caused the change in the turkey's trend during this century?" In view of the anti-hunting sentiment that is so prevalent today, I take a fiendish delight in replying, "It is due, to a significant degree, to the fact that millions of hunters are afield with guns and bows trying to kill them."

Incongruous as that statement may sound, it contains a hard core of truth. Over the last six decades, hunters have contributed, in the form of license fees and taxes on guns and ammunition, untold hundreds of millions of dollars for the protection, restoration, and management of America's wildlife. State game departments, the U.S. Fish and Wildlife Service, and millions of acres of publicly-owned wildlife refuges and hunting areas would not exist, were it not for hunting and hunters. More significantly, the wild turkey, antelope, elk, whitetail deer, and other valuable game species would likely share whatever heavenly abode exists for the ivory-billed woodpecker and the passenger pigeon. Anti-hunting forces, who provide relatively little for wildlife research, restoration, or management, should be hammered into insignificance with those facts.

The recent increase in the number of turkey hunters is largely a result of expansion of the turkey resource. Thousands of neophyte turkey hunters are afield. Many employ the same tactics used in the hunting of deer, tactics that are often counterproductive in hunting turkeys. Many have little or no knowledge of the bird itself, carry no calling devices, have little knowledge of turkey language, and depend upon stalking, luck, and circumstances to bag a turkey. Not only do they pose, to one degree or another, a danger to themselves and other hunters, but they deprive themselves of the supreme esthetic satisfaction derived from calling a bird in close enough to enable a sudden, clean kill with a much reduced chance of crippling loss.

The numerous turkey-related books, tapes, records, organizations, seminars, calling contests, and conventions of the last two decades arose, in part at least, for the purpose of elevating the sport of turkey hunting, educating the turkey hunter, and making the sport safer. It sometimes appears that those events occur often enough to more than fill the need; yet the number of hunting accidents, the proportion of hunters not using calling as a hunting technique, and the amount of illegal or unsportsman-like activity reported suggest that much remains to be accomplished. Hence the need for yet another book by authors of unquestioned exper-tise with shotgun, bow, and camera.

An education that involves only the knowledge and skills essential in being a good turkey hunter and sportsman is woefully inadequate with respect to preserving the turkey and turkey hunting into the indefinite future. Virtually all potential habitat in the United States is expected to be occupied by, or in the early part of, the 21st century. From that point the bird's trend can only be downward unless practical means are found to produce more per unit area. If such means are found, they are unlikely to be capable of counteracting or outpacing the reduction of habitat that is accelerating. The almost inevitable downward trend, the result of human population growth, industrial and urban development, and timber harvesting, shows little possibility of reversal. Incredibly, the trend will even be evident on national forests, despite the fact that data on some have shown that the recreational values of wildlife exceed timber values. (If you, as a turkey hunter, wish to be "shook up," study the U.S. Forest Service's road-building and timber-harvesting proposals for the next decade!)

Turkey hunters, particularly the younger generations, have their work cut out for them. The more knowledge they possess and the more closely and analytically they monitor the programs of game departments, state and federal forestry agencies, and all organizations affecting the environment, the more effectively they can labor for the benefit of the wild turkey.

While this book will surely assist its readers in becoming more skilled and sportsmanlike hunters, it should not, by any means, represent the end of the education of a "turkey nut," whether he be a neophyte or a wizened veteran. There is no ultimate end to knowledge or education. The more one learns about any subject, the more clearly revealed are the areas of ignorance.

Becoming a turkey hunter or attempting to become a better one may foredoom you to a life of despair, frustration, and humiliation. Personally, I hope that you enjoy enough moments of ecstasy, exhilaration, or success to outweigh the aforementioned negatives. But, beware! You have been warned!

R. Wayne Bailey
Retired Chairman–Technical Committee
National Wild Turkey Federation

INTRODUCTION

Bart Jacob has a nice old Belgian Humpback Browning, which I borrowed a while back to photograph for *Field & Stream Magazine*, where I work. After I photographed the gun, I did what anyone who likes guns does: I threw it up to my shoulder and, since it was set up for turkeys with an old Weaver Acu-Sight screwed to the rib, drew a fine bead on the far wall. I pulled back the bolt a couple of times just to hear those well machined parts talk. When I flipped it upside down to take a 360-degree look, I noticed a silver escutcheon on the pistol grip cap. There was engraving on it, so I found my reading glasses and held the gun to the light.

It said:

1st Gobbler, 1976

100th Gobbler, 1986

1st Grand Slam, 1981

That's impressive. Best I recall, the turkey season here in Vermont didn't start much before 1976, and in those early years, birds came hard. Moreover, to take 100 birds in ten years is an extraordinary feat. The Grand Slam might not sound as remarkable as the other two accomplishments, but I know it was, because Old Bart, as I like to call him (a play on the name of his former turkey call business, Old Jake), shot all four subspecies of turkeys on public land.

What that silver plate proves is this: Old Bart knows his turkeys, cold. And that is without knowing the coda to that silver cap of fame, which is that Bart also has taken a Grand Slam with a bow and has killed many more turkeys with other guns. Moreover, he has called in innumerable birds for friends, relatives, and quasi-dignitaries of the turkey world.

With those sort of credentials, Bart Jacob should be in the turkey hunting pantheon, along with Ben Rogers Lee and Rob Keck and the myriad gobbling gurus who strut their stuff in contests and catalogs, at seminars and on tacky TV shows. But Old Jake lacks one thing most of those men have in quantity. It's not knowledge or talent, for sure, but rather a sense of marketing and self-promotion. For all his turkey hunting skills, Old Bart would have a hard time selling ice on the Amazon.

Bart is the consummate idea man and tactician, but the little details of bringing a product to market (or thrusting his name into the limelight) escape him. Two examples come to mind. They tell a bit about his ingenuity (and one must be ingenious to successfully hunt turkeys) and a bit about his manner.

The first involved targets for sighting in a shotgun for turkey hunting. Bart had a huge pile of targets printed up with an outline of a turkey's head and neck, a big red dot on where you should shoot, and a ring circumscribing the picture. According to the prominent type on the target, this ring indicated the kill zone at 40 yards for a full-choked 12-guage shotgun.

Yup, guage, as in *goo-agh*.

When I saw the targets for the first time, I asked Bart if he meant "gauge." His answer was typical Bart: "Ah, you know what I mean."

On the heels of that product came an insulated, collapsible, airline-certified bag for taking game home after a trip. Bart had the bag silk-screened in 6-inch type proclaiming it to be the Old Jake Game Duffle.

Yup, duffle, as in *doof-ley*.

"Do you mean duffel?" I asked Bart. You know the answer: "Ah, you know what I mean."

Sad to say, the doof-ley and the 12-guage target died ignominious deaths.

Not to say Old Bart didn't have some winners under the Old Jake name. His slate call is still my favorite, a lovely looking and sounding call made of rich, heavy leather and Vermont slate. Unlike most of the friction calls on the market today, the One-Hander, as Bart calls it, is of heirloom quality.

The Imitator, a tube call with a silicone diaphragm and an adjustable tone chamber, was almost too good. Not only could it call turkey but also geese, elk, and most predators. I imagine it would call a cab in a city, too.

Old Jake had a few losers along the way, too, products all the marketing skills in the world could not sell. There were the boot camouflage covers; pull-on overshoes designed to hide your soles. And there was a gizmo of bent wire that attached to the front of a bow to hold a branch and its leaves, effectively camouflaging hunter and bow. They both went the way of the doof-ley.

Despite the occasional miscue in marketing, in the mid-eighties, when Old Jake Products was in its prime, the corporate headquarters in Pawlet, Vermont, a converted single-bay garage, was a hot-spot during turkey season. Local hunters and visiting sports would stop in either to show off their birds or to seek advice from the Old Jake. Most seasons, I fell into the second group. Either I couldn't find a bird; or I could find one but he had hung up; or, on one humiliating occasion, I found the bird, called him in, and missed.

No matter where on the road to turkey success I stood, Old Jake always would commiserate and then dispense some good advice. It was delivered not in the Messianic tone of many of the gobbling gurus, who make a living telling us how and where and when to hunt, but in an understated, self-effacing way that made it most palatable. Besides, it was usually dead on.

Which brings me to this book. This is a book written by one Old Jake and a couple of hundred mature birds, with a few doof-leys adding to the chorus. It is a book that covers spring birds and fall birds, problem birds and easy birds (if there is such a thing). It addresses convention turkey hunting with a shotgun and hunting with a bow. In each case the tactical advice here has not been distilled from books that preceded it but gleaned from time in the woods, time spent talking to turkeys.

Old Jake—Old Bart—is the real goods. He is as fine a turkey hunter as I've met, and after 25 years in the outdoor game, I've met them all. He walks the walk and he takes the turkeys. Read this carefully, and you will, too.

And if you need a doof-ley to carry home your bird, give Bart a call.

Lionel Atwill
Dorset, Vermont

Chapter 1

GENERAL INTRODUCTION TO WILD TURKEYS

What is a grand spring hunt? Any hunt that gets hunters back into the woods after a long, cold winter could be considered "grand." Add to this the awakening of life, the greening of plants, the blooming of wildflowers, the sounds and actions of birds and animals in their annual mating rituals, the life-giving spring showers, the early morning mists and fog in the valleys. Include the heart-stopping gobble and a strutting tom turkey and you have the ultimate in hunting—a spring gobbler hunt.

It is this magic time of year when you can be seated with your back against an oak tree, while before you a great dark bird struts in the early morning light. His almost white head is pulled into his chest of iridescent feathers, his fan-like tail is erect, and his wings brush the ground. He takes short steps in one direction, turns and takes more in another, as strange, subtle, yet meaningful sounds reach your ears—sounds of his wing thrusts into the ground. Sharp "tik" like spitting sounds and the booming hum of his "drumming" seems to shake the ground. He is the largest North American game bird, a magnificent creature, notoriously elusive and crafty. Yet, he will respond to your calls by gobbling his territorial challenge and mating call that, under certain conditions, can be heard for a mile or more.

Hunting this highly prized and sought-after trophy, which may be lured to the skillful and lucky hunter, is sure to become one of the most exciting and memorable confrontations you will ever experience. This is what makes a grand spring hunt.

Today, all but a few states hold spring hunts. We now have springtime strutting, wild turkeys in every state in the United States—except Alaska— when only 50 years ago sportsmen and conservationists thought the North American wild turkey was doomed to extinction.

Historians tell us the turkey which we enjoy on our Thanksgiving tables was domesticated somewhere between 150 B.C. and 400 A.D. Also, they say the original domestication occurred either in what is now the southwestern United States or Mexico, but to date no one has determined the exact time and place.

The domesticated turkey is an American Indian treasure which early explorers took back to Europe. But the turkey which we now hunt is not directly descended from domestic turkeys. The common domestic turkey is descended from the Mexican subspecies, Gallopavo gallopavo, and some question whether this subspecies still exists in its wild state.

When wild turkey populations were at their lowest in the early 1900's many outdoor people assumed that releasing domestic turkeys into the wild was the answer to the declining population problem. It wasn't.

The first attempts at restoring wild turkeys to their former glory took several routes before the present path was found. They tried releasing pen-raised domestic turkeys. They incubated eggs from wild hens, and released these pen-reared birds. The combinations to reintroduce birds back into the wild seemed endless. Unfortunately, though some systems had limited successes, they held no promise of permanent increases in turkey populations.

Then someone, and we don't know exactly who, began catching and transplanting wild turkeys to areas where the native stock was either depleted or had been eliminated. And it worked.

The "trap-and-transfer" method worked so well that birds were quickly restored to their former range and also to parts of the U.S. where they never existed before. The turkey is native to the Americas and there is no historical evidence that it ever existed elsewhere. Transplanted to West Germany though, it now thrives there. One question now being asked is: "Are there other parts of the world suitable for turkey transplanting?"

This may seem over-simplified to many who followed the reintroduction of the American wild turkey. The knowledge necessary to trap and transplant turkeys was acquired over decades of trial and error by dedicated biologists and conservation-minded sportsmen. Common sense tells us that all turkeys are the same species—a species is defined as a

A wildlife technician grabs a just-netted turkey from a net used to trap birds over bait. The procedure is employed to collect data and to transfer turkeys to suitable habitat elsewhere.

group which can breed and reproduce within itself—and all wild turkey subspecies can and have successfully been interbred with all other subspecies. Thus, they should all behave the same even if centuries of separation gave them slightly different physical appearances. Not so;

Recording the vital statistics of each trapped bird helps to determine how a local population is faring and can indicate whether there is a problem in the area and how it might be solved.

nature is not wasteful. Seemingly insignificant racial differences have their survival values.

The Western birds, Rio Grandes and Merriam's, were the first transplants—with the Black Hills of South Dakota and Wyoming receiving transplanted turkeys before mid-century. These were the first transplants because they were the easiest to capture; they could be induced to walk under a drop net which made catching them comparatively easy. Eastern birds resisted capture by this method, and it wasn't until about

Healthy birds are boxed for shipment. States such as New Jersey have reintroduced turkeys by obtaining them from states with abundant populations.

1950 that modern cannon nets proved successful in capturing them. When Vermont planned its restoration program, the only question biologists needed to answer was, "Do we have suitable habitat?" and not, "How do we obtain birds?"

There is now a growing concern among biologists over wild turkey hybridization, whether it is accidental or intentional. If the mixing of genes should produce a bird better able to survive in the wild it would be a boon to the turkey's future. But if gene mixing went the opposite way and reduced the wild turkey's ability to survive it could be a disaster.

In many areas, well-meaning sportsmen and Fish & Game Departments released semi-domestic or pen-reared birds into the wild. Since the 1950's, however, most game agencies have used only pure native stock for transplanting. A few states, including an important turkey state (Pennsylvania), continued programs of game-farm releases through the 1970's. Many state agencies will not release trapped birds into areas where local sportsmen have stocked pen-raised birds.

Every day new discoveries are made. Numerous organizations and an ever increasing number of Fish & Game Department biologists throughout the country are working toward increasing our knowledge of this wild and hard to hunt bird—the bird that Benjamin Franklin suggested be named our National Bird.

Chapter 2

DESCRIPTION OF THE GOBBLER

In a recent television show, a man lying hidden behind a log captured a wild turkey gobbler with his hand. If a turkey is as wild and hard to hunt as most turkey hunters claim, how could that be true?

Not all gobblers were, or are, wary and hard to hunt. Some were more trusting of man than the average present day wild turkey is. Wayne Bailey and Kermit T. Rinell in their book the *History and Management of the Wild Turkey in West Virginia* quote from Hildreth's observations in 1836 on the Hughes River as follows.

. . . "about the period of my becoming an inhabitant in the valley of the Ohio, the wild turkey was found in astonishing abundance; many hundreds being, on favorite feeding grounds, often seen in one flock. They were so little scared at the sight of their natural enemy, man, that they often entered his fields close to the door of his cabin, and partook of the corn he had thrown out to his hogs . . . At this period, a "backwoodsman" had established himself on or near to, the eastern branches of Hew's (Hughes) River between Marietta and Clarksburg, Virginia, he had erected a cabin and opened a small "clearing." In the autumn, he enclosed a lot near his door, in which to feed and fatten his hogs. A flock of about thirty turkeys, attracted by the corn, came regularly, morning and evening, to partake with the hogs which, being themselves in those early days, well fed, when every kind of food was abundant, made no opposition to their visits. The owner . . . , standing in the door, however, every day shot one or two of the unsuspecting birds: seeing no person near, they were but little alarmed at the report of the rifle, nor were they frightened away by the sight of their dead companions. In this manner, without leaving the door of his hut, the owner, at the time of my information, had killed twenty seven out of thirty turkeys."

Indians, of course, hunted North American wild turkeys long before white men arrived here, but there were many turkeys and few Indians.

We know Indians hunted turkeys because archaeologists found tools made from bones of wild turkey gobblers reportedly dating as far as 5,000 years ago.

Not only were wild turkeys a staple in the diet of early Indians, but parts of turkeys such as beards, spurs, and feathers were used as adornments and tools. When white men arrived in North America they hunted turkeys for food. Many early accounts speak of wild turkeys as being rather tame and easy to hunt as was most other game.

In the years following, most tame and easy-to-hunt turkeys were killed in incidents similar to the pig-pen episode mentioned earlier. The turkeys wild enough to avoid being killed became the future breeding stock and passed their characteristics to succeeding generations.

Even today, a wide variation in wildness exists among turkeys of the same region and even in a single brood. Mature gobblers are warier than young gobblers or "jakes" as they are often called. But the greater wariness of a mature gobbler may be an illusion since it is quite possible jakes are merely immature and their group contains both the wary and unwary, while with mature gobblers the unwary have already been eliminated. Obviously, the least wary grace the plates of the majority of inexperienced hunters who need only employ the crudest of hunting tactics to kill them.

But others, those exhibiting extreme wariness or wildness, are more than a challenge for even the most sophisticated of hunters using the newest equipment and hunting tactics. This wildness, when it comes to association with man, is based on just that—a turkey's association with man.

In areas where turkeys are hunted over bait or food plots, or where they are hunted at long range by rifle, they are less wary of an imperfectly camouflaged man or an imperfect imitation of a turkey call. Where turkeys are hunted daily, however, by sportsmen using the same type of turkey call, as they are on some public hunting grounds in the South, they will sometimes flee from an expert hunter who is perfectly camouflaged and executing perfect yelps from his artificial call.

If you are fortunate enough to hunt in areas where there are many turkeys and few hunters, such as the Black Hills of Wyoming, you can often take a turkey while dressed in street clothes. Since you can use a rifle in Wyoming, you need not get closer than 100 or so yards if you are a good shot. And the Merriam's which inhabit this area have not been hunted enough to acquire fear of a man that far away. Rather, they are more inclined to run from stopped pickup trucks from which most of the shooting occurs.

I once shot a strutting Merriam's gobbler, following which two mature gobblers stepped out of the underbrush and began pummeling the fallen monarch. They then squared off to see who would replace the boss I just killed, while I stood in plain view and watched the escapade. If you exposed yourself to a strutting gobbler in New York's Washington County during the spring, even though the distance was several hundred yards, the gobbler would cease strutting and race for cover.

This is a result of learned behavior, less association with man and less hunting pressure in the West, more association with man and heavier hunting pressure in the East, rather than any genetic defect within any subspecies. You might say this is also true of a deer, rabbit, etc. Why does a turkey become harder to bag than a deer or rabbit? Because of its survival equipment, the way it uses that equipment, and the quickness with which it learns when to use it.

A turkey's hearing is as acute as most woodland animals. The only thing it lacks is a strong sense of smell. Its eyes, situated near the top of its head, have a 270-degree field of view. Also, like many other birds, the resolving power of a turkey's eyes allows it to see more detail in a shorter period of time. In other words it has great ability to discern movement. Although turkeys lack good night vision they see color, as can other birds, equal to or better than man.

An adult turkey can outrun a dog. Yet, it can thunder into the air and, given enough elevation, soar a mile before alighting.

But most important of all these survival characteristics are the reactions which come from its nut-size brain. There is little curiosity. If something isn't quite right, a turkey is gone. Rarely are there second thoughts. Even if there was nothing there at all. And this coupled with his

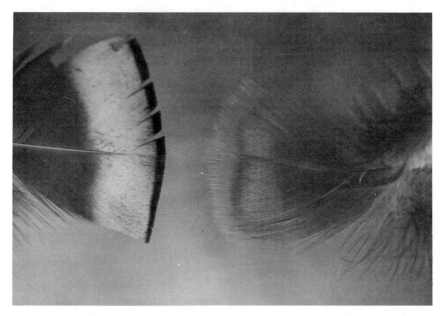

This picture shows the differences in the breast feathering of a male (left) and female.

ability to "learn," in a manner similar to that of a dog, by association, means there is no need to repeat the lesson, once is enough. All this coupled with thousands of years of the fittest surviving, passing down their instincts to succeeding generations, has made the wild turkey gobbler a worthy opponent for any hunter.

It would be a great help to you if you could tell at a glance the difference between a wary and unwary bird, but it is not possible. Often experts are confused, though less often than most of us.

Experts can determine the sex of a turkey from the time of hatching by examining the cloacal cavity. But there is no easy way for the average hunter to determine the difference in the sex of a young turkey until after the first winter molt which is not usually completed until November. It's during this molt, the third the young turkeys have gone through since hatching, that the breast feathers of the males (jakes) become black-tipped. At this stage the breast and back of a young gobbler appear darker than the same area on a hen.

Shortly after hatching, males may have slightly larger feet and longer necks than females, but even experts can't determine sex at this point in a turkey's life using size of feet alone without making an occasional

The primary wing-tip feathers reveal (from left) a mature bird, an immature turkey, and a strutting gobbler.

mistake. By summer though, it becomes more obvious. By late fall, the feet of both sexes are approximately equal in size to those of adults. The foot of a male is in excess of 4½ inches long if you are measuring a clear imprint; the foot of a female, no more than 4½ inches.

The easiest way to distinguish young birds from adults is by examining the wing tips. The tip of the outermost primary wing feather of an adult bird is rounded and its white barring extends the length of the feather. In young birds this feather is more pointed and the outer 1-2 inches lack the white barring. Biologists take this one step further and by measuring certain wing-tip feathers can determine the actual age of a young-of-the-year bird in days and use this information in setting seasons.

The tips of the primaries of a breeding gobbler are often well worn due to his strutting actions, at which time they are dragged on the ground as the bird walks.

Other ways of telling young birds from old and males from females include shape and color of head, color of feet, and shape of tail.

The head of a hen is small compared with a gobbler. Her neck is fully feathered. Small fine feathers can be found over her entire head which will be gray to blue-gray in color. The only red on a hen's head is the

The long center feathers of the turkey fan indicate an immature bird. This is an easy way for a hunter to tell a jake from a mature gobbler.

membrane or dewlap under her chin which will only show vividly when back-lighted. A young gobbler's head has scattered hair-like feathers, and is generally an obvious red color. The head of an old gobbler is larger due to his larger skull, the size of his fleshy caruncles and appendages, and depending on the season and his activity at the time observed, will vary from snow white to blue and bright red or combinations of all three. The head of a breeding gobbler can vary in colors in a matter of moments due to variations in blood supply to its tissues, caruncles, and snood. The snood, which is noticeable on a newly hatched bird and is present, but small, on a hen, varies on the gobbler during the breeding season from a short erect position above his bill to a long finger-like limp position hanging down one side of his face. The anatomy of a gobbler's head and the difficulties in shaping it present formidable problems to many taxidermists.

If you see the head color of an approaching gobbler in the spring and it looks like a snowball, the chances are it is a mature bird, but not always. A breeding jake can have the same color. By the same token, if the head color is red, the chances are it is a jake, but a non-dominant, mature bird can fool you.

Young birds of both sexes have feet and legs of grayish-brown, at maturity they are pink and in older birds light red.

This fan is from a mature turkey. Note the difference between this and the fan of the jake.

The tails of young birds change with the first winter molt when new feathers are grown, beginning from the center of the tail outward. Normally 4-6 pairs of the central tail feathers are replaced before the onset of cold weather. The youngest birds have a gap in their tail as the first new center feathers have yet to fully form. Reduced sunlight at the end of fall halts molting and it does not resume until spring. Hence, a bird is not fully mature until reduced sunlight halts molting in the second fall of its life. Early born and late-born birds can be distinguished by the number of feathers replaced. In the second fall of its life a turkey has a full, even "fan" and may then be regarded as mature.

The criteria most fish and game departments use to separate the sexes for purposes of harvesting turkeys is, "You can only harvest bearded birds." A gobbler without a beard is a real rarity, but a hen with a beard is not uncommon. However, this method of defining the difference between males and females is reliable enough for most purposes.

Beard lengths may vary, thus the length of spur is used to determine a gobbler's age. The normal rate of beard growth is 4-to-5 inches per year for the first 2-3 years. An adult two-year-old gobbler will usually have a beard 8-to-10 inches long. It has an amber tip still evident and will not yet

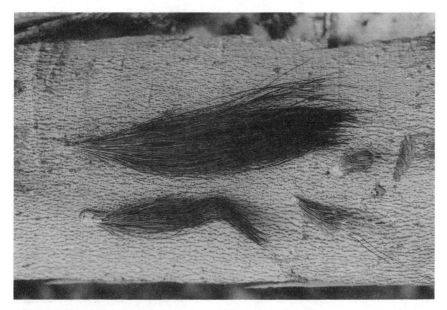

At top left is the beard of a mature gobbler, and to its right is the stubby beard of a jake of the year. At bottom left is the beard of a jake in its second spring, and to its right the wispy beard of a hen. Most but not all hens are beardless.

show any wear from dragging on the ground. By its third year, though, the amber tip is gone and the individual beard hairs are chisel-tipped from dragging and wear. Thus a gobbler with a 10-inch beard that still has amber tips is a two-year-old, while a gobbler with a 10-inch or longer beard that is not amber tipped is most certainly a three-year-old or older bird. Some gobblers have separate multiple beards and are listed in the record books as non-typical.

A button spur is present at hatching on both sexes and has grown noticeably larger on young gobblers by fall. The spur will usually be ¼-to-½ inch long when the gobbler is a year old and ¾-to-⅞ inch long when he is two years old. After two years the spur tends to become curved and unless worn becomes sharper and increases slightly in length. Spurs rarely exceed 1¾ inch in length even in very old birds. Some recent studies show a gobbler's spurs continue to grow throughout its life, reaching 1½ inches at about six years of age. The same studies indicate the length and condition of a gobblers spur is a much better indicator of his age than any other criteria. Merriam's turkeys, due to their rocky

These spurs (from left) indicate a very old turkey, a bird two to three years old, and a jake.

habitat, tend to wear off their spurs more than others. The study also indicates that after three years of age a spur grows at a decreased rate. There are also instances of multiple spurs, as well as lack of spurs, on gobblers.

All these methods of differentiating between hens and gobblers and mature and immature birds is of primary concern to fish and game personnel, to serious students, and to experienced turkey hunters. For those of you who are just entering into the sport it is enough to note that if it gobbles in the spring and occasionally pauses to strut with its tail fanned out to its full circular size when coming into your calls . . . it's a gobbler.

Chapter 3

FOUR AMERICAN SUBSPECIES

As mentioned earlier, there's only one species of turkey and it includes all domestic and wild strains. Poultry scientists have named different domestic strains and zoologists have given names to different wild geographic subspecies. (The terms subspecies, geographic strains, and races are synonymous.) Subspecies, or races, are similar to races in humans, in a biological sense. Regardless of subspecific names, all turkeys can interbreed successfully, and are therefore of the same species. Basically, there are four subspecies of wild turkey you can hunt today within the United States—the Eastern (Meleagris gallopavo silvestris), Merriam's (Meleagris gallopavo merriami), Rio Grande (Meleagris gallopavo intermedia), and the Florida (Meleagris gallopavo osceola).

In the Eastern U.S. there is the Eastern turkey whose range extends from the Canadian border to north Florida. Florida turkeys are strictly native to Florida, but as with all subspecies with overlapping range, no clear line can be drawn on a map separating the Eastern and Florida turkeys.

In the Western U.S. we have the Merriam's and the Rio Grande turkeys. The Merriam's is a bird of the Rocky Mountains and the Rio Grande is a bird of the open grasslands of the Southwest and southward into eastern Mexico.

A subspecies is defined according to the geographic area in which it lives. Each subspecies differs, however, at least slightly, from all other by color, size, or minor anatomical criteria.

The spread wing feathers of the bird at left clearly show the barring of the secondaries. A Florida bird at right lacks this barring.

An Eastern bird at left shows dark tips, whereas a Western bird has light tips.

The Eastern race is indistinguishable from the Florida subspecies unless a specimen from each can be examined in hand. The Florida subspecies, like the Eastern, has brown tail tips and brown-tipped iridescent rump feathers or upper tail coverts. The Florida is also slightly smaller than the other three races.

The pure strain Rio Grande has white tail tips and cinnamon colored greater tail covert tips.

The Merriam's has creamy-white tail tips similar to the Rio Grande, and white rump feather tips which with the light-colored secondary wing feathers blend together to make a white patch in stark contrast to the dark body feathers. It and the Eastern bird are the largest of the four races.

The most obvious difference between wild and domestic turkeys is that wild birds are more streamlined. One reason is the tarsal bone—the nude looking, lower leg bone reaching from the feathered thigh to the four toed section of the foot resting on the ground—is longer than in domestic birds. Also, wild birds have thinner thighs. Domestic birds are bred to produce heavy, meaty bodies for the table. When compared with wild birds their thighs are puffy. Also, a wild bird's head is smaller, the neck longer, more serpentine. Also, the rest of a domestic bird's body looks heavier than a wild bird's.

The Florida turkey is different than the Eastern because it has a longer tarsus. It also has a smaller head, and a more streamlined and somewhat smaller body. The first one I saw surprised me.

I was hunting in Florida with my friend, Dave Harbour. He told me where to sit and left me to call my own bird. I called sparingly, but couldn't get a bird to come in. I decided to explore the area and look for sign. Returning later, I rounded a palmetto and saw a young gobbler standing in front of the bush I called from. Obviously, it came to see where the hen that was calling, went. But when I rounded the bush, it looked like a heron. Its head was up, and it was so streamlined in comparison to the Eastern birds which I was familiar with, that I mistook it for a long-legged shore bird. I was deceived just long enough that it was running before I realized it was a turkey and could get my gun to my shoulder.

The white barring on the wing primaries of a Florida bird does not stretch from edge to edge the way it does on an Eastern turkey. It is broken. And the barring on the wing secondaries is almost non-existent, while it is distinct on the Eastern bird. Also the secondaries on a mature

Habitat varies enormously throughout the country. Shown here is a typical hunting area for Florida birds—a cypress swamp.

Florida gobbler look furry and soft, not as hard and smooth looking as an Eastern bird's secondaries. Many who hunt all four subspecies claim the Florida bird is the most iridescent.

The most obvious difference between the two Eastern and Western races is that the Western birds' tail tips run from a white to a creamy-white. Biologists claim there is a difference in tarsal length, but with the exception of the Florida bird, I can't tell the difference. Often, there's some reference made to a difference in size between Eastern and Western birds. I have killed 21-pound Merriam's and that's a big bird anywhere.

Where the ranges of the two Western subspecies overlap, you are apt to see rump or upper tail covert feather tips, particularly of the Rio Grande, ranging from creamy-white to deep cinnamon. This, of course, makes correct determination of each subspecies ancestry difficult. This is why biologists consider the subspecies division as geographical rather than biological. This melting of one subspecies into another also occurs where natural ranges of the Eastern and Florida birds overlap. To add to the confusion, some states have transplanted birds outside their ancestral habitat; thus combination and multiple races occur in some areas where wild flocks were reintroduced by transplanting.

Typical Eastern habitat is often hilly, with open areas bordered by hardwoods.

Eastern birds prefer feeding in nut-bearing hardwoods where they eat the nuts, insects, and plants found in the hardwood duff. In the spring, before mating starts, I've noticed they tend to follow the retreating snowline as it melts up hillsides. When doing this they feed heavily on sprouting nuts and green matter.

During the mating season, of course, mature gobblers rarely eat; they draw nourishment from their fatty breast or sponge. I've examined the contents of many mature gobbler crops and found most of them empty. In the few cases where I found food, it was usually small amounts of grasses and sprouts. But for some reason I've often found jack-in-the-pulpit in the crops of Eastern spring gobblers and the blossoms of the wild crocus in the crops of Merriam's.

Florida birds live in a different environment. For one thing, Florida doesn't have many mature hardwoods. The Florida gobbler usually roosts in Cypress "heads" which abound there and which are surrounded by water. (This is where the phrase, "that a turkey feels safe if it can hear its droppings hit the water while it's on the roost" originated.) Cypress heads are Cypress tree clumps growing in pools of water that dot the flat areas on which palmettos abound. The Florida turkey's main food supply are the grasses growing among the palmettos and the insects living

Not all Florida turkey hunting is done in muck and mire. Open areas such as shown here are also good, especially with nearby cypress cover in the background.

there. In recent years, ranchers have burned these palmettos to increase the amount of grasses available for the large cattle raising operations in the area. This, in turn, has increased the grass and insects for turkeys. Also, turkeys feed often in "hammocks" of the area. These are places of higher ground where scrub oak and other such trees grow.

This environment produces a long-legged version of the Eastern bird which runs around in water and whose presence is often first detected by hunters who hear them splashing.

In contrast, it is often said that you can't call an Eastern bird across a small brook. And Western birds may not see as much water in their lifetimes as Eastern birds see in a year. The Rio Grande, for instance, lives in open country that is dry and has few big trees. A Rio Grande spends its days in open grassland that Eastern birds would avoid at all costs. Rio Grandes also roost in trees barely six feet tall. They use tall trees when available but their ancestral range has few tall trees, other than an occasional clump of cottonwoods. The bird will roost within 100 yards of an all-night bistro if it's the only place with a roosting facility.

As for food preferences, the Rio Grande feeds on the grasses of the plains and the insects which live there.

Cactus and wide open spaces mark the habitat of the Rio Grande wild turkey—a setting far different from the thick cover in some other regions.

The rock and canyon country of the West can be home for flocks of Merriam's. This terrain makes for tough hunting, but the Merriam's is a beautiful trophy for any turkey hunter.

The Merriam's lives in mountainous country often well stocked with ponderosa pine. The seeds of ponderosa and piñon pines are prime food sources. The Black Hills of South Dakota and Wyoming are an excellent example of the habitat these birds prefer. In many respects this area resembles some of the less productive Eastern agricultural areas, such as New Jersey's pinelands, where farming was tried and quickly abandoned. The only difference, to casual observers, is that the Western home of the Merriam's is much drier. The Merriam's is a distant relative of our domestic bronze turkeys and when photographs of Merriam's appear in outdoor magazines, Eastern turkey hunters often mistake them for farmyard bronze gobblers.

All turkeys are omnivorous and opportunistic in their food choices. In one study conducted in Virginia more than 354 species of plants were found in their diet. This is in addition to insect and other animal life they consume. A wild turkey may have the most varied diet of any animal known. Studies of dietary needs of turkeys indicate "if it is slow enough to catch and small enough to swallow, turkeys will more than likely make a meal of it."

There are two other North American subspecies: the Mexican turkey (Meleagris gallopavo gallopavo), and Gould's turkey (Meleagris gallopavo mexicana), and a genus found in parts of the Yucatan Peninsula, the Ocellated turkey (Agriocharis ocellata).

The Mexican (Gallopavo gallopavo), as mentioned earlier, may no longer exist in the wild.

The Gould's occurs mainly in the Sierra Madre Mountains of northwestern Mexico. A few occur, though, in the San Luis Mountains of New Mexico. New Mexico lists the Gould's as an endangered species and no hunting of it is permitted.

Gould's is the largest subspecies of wild turkey. It has longer feet, legs, wings, and tail. Also, it weighs more and is taller. In coloration, the Gould's iridescence is more greenish. The outer tips of its tail coverts and tail feathers are nearly pure white, which contrasts with the Merriam's buff color.

Ocellated turkeys are said to have the longest spurs of all turkeys. They don't have beards and their heads are unfeathered, much like the head of a buzzard or bustard. The head color is blue with red caruncles. Their feathers are described as "parrot-like greens and blues." The males "sing" rather than gobble.

Chapter 4
LIFE CYCLE AND LANGUAGE OF THE GOBBLER

The gobbler's life begins in the egg. It is here he hears his first sounds—his mother's soft clucks as she urges the hatching. The "cluck" is a short, single syllable sound that can vary greatly in sharpness and volume. It is used singly or repeated with variations in tempo depending upon its meaning. After the entire brood is hatched, this soft clucking continues as the chicks become imprinted to the hen through an associative learning process. Within a day, the gobbler and his brothers and sisters leave the nest and continue the learning process.

The sounds of the poults are for the most part "peeps" much like any other kind of chick, although their language at this early stage is nearly as complicated as adults. During the young gobbler's early adventures, he learns the meaning of different variations of his mother's clucks, yelps, or whines. He is programmed to respond quickly when her clucks sharpen. He is also programmed to respond immediately when she makes a slightly louder, very sharp cluck, which is the danger sound or "alarm putt."

The alarm putt is also usually given in a somewhat rapid series. A single putt is not necessarily an alarm sound. The poults respond appropriately to the different calls of the hen.

As the gobbler grows, he will start to yelp. The cluck and the yelp are the most common turkey sounds.

The "yelp" is usually a two-syllable sound with the first note being higher than the second. It can also vary from the melodic to the coarse and sometimes will consist of a single note. The yelp is usually given in an evenly spaced series, the tempo of which will vary depending on mean-

Hens and jakes in Vermont. Knowing the life cycle of the turkey will make the hunter more aware of his quarry's habits, and thereby make him a more successful hunter.

ing. Gobblers have more dragged out yelps which are slower in rhythm than those of hens.

The young gobbler will also whine or whistle when left behind or separated from the others. This sound is known as the kee-kee and is hard to differentiate between male and female poults.

The "kee-kee" is a whistling sound usually consisting of three notes rising in pitch and will often vary in intensity as to the anxiety over the young birds' separation from each other or their mother. The farther apart they are, the more frantic the calling.

When yelps are added, they will sometimes indicate whether they are being made by a young gobbler or hen (the gobbler's yelp is often coarser) and this is called the "kee-kee run."

During this period, he also hears his mother's loud assembly yelps. She usually uses these after her assembly clucks have failed to unite the brood.

In the morning, when first waking on the roost, he uses the very soft tree yelp along with soft clucks to greet the new day and his family before flying down. The "tree yelp," made by all turkeys, is a very soft yelp that sounds somewhat muffled as it is made by the awakening bird. Once on the ground he uses kee-kees and kee-kee runs to regroup with the flock.

Eventually, because of genetic programming, he begins making his distinctive sound—the gobble. At first it is a pitiful excuse for a gobble, often emerging from a yelp or blending into one.

The "gobble" needs little description except that it is a sound made only by the male and it will vary in tone and pitch depending upon the bird. Generally speaking, an older bird has a more melodic, distinct gobble. However, some jakes in their first spring can gobble as well as any adult. Young gobblers in the fall will always have a short, broken gobble, often interspersed with kee-kees and yelps.

As fall approaches, the gobble becomes more recognizable. The jakes seem to practice their gobbles and use them to assemble as a group within the flock. They mimic each other, and one gobble is often followed by those of other jakes. During the summer and fall jakes also do some strutting (they may do this also as poults) and mock fighting. This is instinctive and not yet serious. The pecking order is being established, with the stronger chasing the weaker.

By fall hunting season, jakes are noticeably larger than their sisters and mother and have a stronger affinity for other young males within the flock.

The sounds made by the flock that the young gobbler responds to and makes at this time are clucks and their variations, yelps and their variations, kee-kees and kee-kee runs, attempted gobbles, and purrs.

"Purrs" are whirring or fluttering sounds. When short and musical, they indicate contentment. A longer, louder more evenly pitched purr denotes aggressive threatening to another turkey. If a dominant jake calls and another, sub-dominant, bird answers, the dominant bird often uses this aggravated purr to express his superiority. It is also made by fighting gobblers.

During late fall and early winter, young gobblers normally leave the family unit to form separate flocks, but continue to adjust the pecking order. Hens of all ages generally remain together until spring "break-up" and dispersal. The young gobbler now seldom uses the kee-kee, relying instead on the yelp, purr, and an occasional gobble to communicate. From now on he is usually less vocal than his sisters. He also develops a distinctive gobbler cluck which is sometimes used singly, sometimes in series. This cluck sounds like a "pop." It is often described as sounding like an acorn dropping on a hollow log.

In the West, wintering birds travel many miles to find easy meals, such

A Vermont jake, or immature bird. It's fairly easy to tell jakes from adults by their longer center tail feathers and because the beard and spurs are not fully developed.

as cattle feed on a large ranch. A similar situation exists in Vermont's Mettowee Valley. There, turkeys travel long distances to feed on undigested corn in cow manure spread on snow-covered fields by farmers. In both situations the young gobbler often finds himself in a group within a relatively large mixed flock.

As winter progresses, the length of days increase. The longer days produce changes in turkeys. Mature gobblers begin gobbling on the roost and continue during the early morning hours. Jakes imitate and answer these gobbles. The mature gobblers also start to strut, but when young gobblers start imitating the strutting, the older birds come at them, beating them, and chasing them off, in some instances, a group of jakes may dominate an older gobbler.

Thus chastised, the young gobbler may turn to his brothers. Even here, the old mock fights suddenly become meaningful. And when, at last in exasperation, he turns to his sisters or mother in hopes of finding someone he can dominate, the old gobbler is on him once again. The once tight family flock is now intolerant of him. He is forced to stay at a distance alone or with some of his brothers and cousins.

For a while he still mimics the gobbles of mature gobblers, but later he will be afraid to do even that as he gets pummeled more and more as the breeding season progresses.

He now detects some new variations in hen language. The hens now make more excited, choppy yelps, cackles, and cutts, all triggering excitement in the young gobbler. He is now like all young males, feeling the urge to procreate the race, but socially restricted from participating, and chastised severely if he tries.

The "cutt" is a very sharp, usually high pitched note, normally given in a rapid series. The "cackle" is hard to define, but in my opinion, it is a very rapid series of cutts made with varying rhythm and pitch within a given series. These calls are generally broken up with excited yelping.

The young gobbler is so naturally programmed by centuries of breeding habits that he may gobble every time he hears an excited cutt or cackle even after being frightened by a hunter.

Several times, I have called in jakes which eventually spotted me, then putted and ran. As they were running full-tilt away from me I would cutt and cackle on my box call, receiving gobbles from them in response. On each occasion, I was able to do this several times as they disappeared.

Merriam's turkeys on a snow-covered hillside.

However, the majority of young gobblers learn their survival skills quickly.

Sometimes after the mature gobblers in an area are taken by hunters, a jake gets to mate with hens. According to R. Wayne Bailey, there is now some evidence that often jakes, within the Eastern subspecies, are infertile even when they are fully capable of mating.

Scientific study shows that a hen mated with a mature gobbler produces fertilized eggs up to 56 days after mating. This means, a hen who mates with a mature gobbler once can lay all the eggs necessary for a first hatching without again mating with a gobbler.

There is also evidence that should the first nest be destroyed or abandoned and a second nest started, the hen need not mate with a gobbler again. She can still produce the necessary fertilized eggs from her first mating. In nature, where nothing is left to chance, the hen may continue to accept the gobbler's advances even after there is no biological need. Therefore, much to the chagrin of the turkey hunter, if the hen loses her nest after incubation has begun, she will normally return to a gobbler before attempting to re-nest (recycling of the reproductive cycle).

Hunters often cull those jakes who become opportunistic and fall for artificial calling. Those surviving have started an associative learning process which later makes them more difficult trophies.

A young gobbler, in the second fall of his life, has a full fan, an obvious beard and a noticeable spur. He has become a trophy in many ways. He is, at this time, difficult to hunt and remains so—except for his vulnerability during the next breeding season. He yelps when lost or is at a distance from other gobblers in his bachelor group, but he uses his cluck for most of his communications. I have heard him use a whining yelp when approaching other turkeys. Also, during the summer, fall, and winter he occasionally gobbles.

As spring approaches again, he becomes aggressive, fighting with his fellow bachelors to determine who will be the area's boss gobbler for that breeding season.

He may tolerate younger males only if they make no signs of breeding (gobbling, strutting, or approaching hens). He now starts his melodious booming gobble at daybreak and continues gobbling into the early morning hours. His gobble and his strut are for the purpose of attracting hens and are also an expression of territoriality. While the gobble is probably used for both, the main purpose of the strut is to "impress" the hen (elicit mating behavior).

During his strut, a gobbler at close quarters can be heard "spitting" and "drumming." The two sounds are apparently a part of the same action. The first part, the spit, is a sharp "tik" with a soft "T" followed by the drum. The drum is caused by a vibration of the breast musculature that resounds through the crop which is inflated with air and apparently serves as a sounding chamber. This vibration produces a humming that sounds like a taut rubber band being plucked. This humming in the right circumstances can sound like a soft "boom." (I can hear the spit farther than the drum.) The drum is accompanied by vibrations of the wing and tail feathers which at one time were believed to have caused the sound.

The gobbler, by his actions, seeks to attract hens to him. Often as not, they move toward each other. The hen's habit of also meandering about, feeding, and carrying on her daily activities, except when actually breeding, tends to lead the gobbler about. This may be why, when a skillful hunter attempts calling the gobbler to him, he can do so successfully.

Before hunting season, hens are quite social and often vocalize. However, as they are bred and have to sneak off daily, without the gobbler noticing, to lay eggs, they become quieter and communicate with softer calls. This becomes particularly true when hunters appear in the woods. With hunting pressure, the gobbler limits his gobbles, and in some instances learns to gobble deceptively soft. With extreme pressure the gobbler and his hens stay in touch by sight and subtle sounds like footsteps, scratching, and his strutting sounds.

Only when all his hens have begun setting and deserted him does he become foolish. For several days he will gobble with abandon, trying to regain his hens. However, he eventually reverts to his summer, fall, and winter habits, perhaps finding a gobbler or two of his own age with whom to associate. He usually ignores the young turkey families that appear in early summer. For the most part, he relies on his keen eyesight, his cluck, and an occasional short series of yelps, to stay in touch with his bachelor buddies.

Bear in mind that this chapter has necessarily presented a simplified picture of the turkey's complex life and language. For a better grasp of turkey language, I recommend *The Master Wild Turkey Tape*, narrated by Sam Nenno and Tom Stuckey, produced by Penn's Woods Products; and the tape series entitled *Real Turkeys*, by Lovett Williams and David Austin.

Chapter 5

TURKEY CALLS:
Pros and Cons

Although turkey "language" may be quite simple compared with ours, we probably have only a vague understanding of the meaning of its various sounds. Nevertheless, people can imitate these sounds—or "talk turkey"—well enough to call tens of thousands of the birds to the gun each year. Some people can do this with their own voice, but for most of us who can't, calling devices are available. These devices allow us to entice gobblers to us in the spring. The toms often answer with booming gobbles. When near the caller he often "spits" and "drums," while puffing himself up in glorious display.

In my opinion, calling gobblers in the spring is the only way to hunt turkeys. There are other ways of killing turkeys—with rifles at long range, shooting them in their roosts (which may be illegal and always considered unethical), or just plain waylaying them. But once you successfully call a turkey to you, with all the anticipation and heart-stopping anxiety that can sometimes last for hours, you should become a true turkey hunting enthusiast and enjoy all the fervor connected with it.

Calling devices have been successfully used on turkeys for centuries. There is evidence that Indians used such devices as peg and slates or wingbone yelpers. In more modern times, diaphragm type calls were developed.

There are two basic types of calls: those producing sound by friction and those producing sound by moving air through an orifice or over a

An assortment of box calls, considered by many hunters to be the only way to seduce a gobbling turkey. These calls include hinge-lid models at left and right, scratch calls at center.

diaphragm. Within these two types there are many variations and each has its advantages and disadvantages. Following is a description of many of these calls with some of their good points and shortcomings.

Among friction calls, the one we think of first is the big box call, also called the hinged-lid box call. A good box call produces the truest calls and they are relatively easy to master. Sound is produced by a wooden lid as it is moved across sides of similar wood, or even different woods, which form an enclosed sound chamber. A hinged-lid box is easy to operate, and a good box produces all turkey sounds except the kee-kee or whistle of young turkeys.

The sounds from a box are true enough to fool many knowledgeable turkey hunters. I have often had hunters in my shop say they mistook real turkeys for a box call in the hands of a novice caller. The hinged lid box is large, somewhat fragile, and with some exceptions, noisy if improperly carried.

The scratch box is smaller and more compact than the hinged-lid box. It also is capable of making very true turkey sounds. Because of its size and because the striking surfaces are unattached or separate from each other, it's easier to carry and not as prone to making accidental noises as

Slate calls are the favorite of a growing number of hunters. They're relatively easy to master and produce lifelike sounds.

the hinged-lid box. It is not as easy to use as the hinged-lid box, however, because the angles and movements of the striking surfaces can be mismanaged. And like the hinged-lid box, the scratch box also is not capable of the kee-kee, nor will it make the gobble. Both boxes can be used softly as well as having relatively good range or volume. The most obvious disadvantage of most boxes is that they require two hands to operate.

Peg and slate calls come in many varieties. They also provide some of the truest turkey sounds—particularly at close range. Peg and slate calls are operated by striking or moving a peg made of wood or plastic over a slate surface providing sounds much as those made on the old school blackboard. There are fixed and adjustable slates, like those mounted in a frame, and hand-held or unmounted slates. These slates are simple to use, but provide only soft sounds. They are capable of producing all turkey talk except the kee-kee and the gobble but normally require two hands to use.

There are resonating slates that allow a free edge of the slate to vibrate within a sound chamber. These provide a greater variety of sounds including the kee-kee and increased volume, closely approaching that of box calls. The free vibrating surface is provided for in several ways:

Pegs, or strikers, come in a variety of styles. The most common materials are wood and Plexiglass or plastic.

through large holes drilled in the slate; through a second free-edged slate attached to the first, and through a special mounting arrangement providing a free edge.

Most slates require two hands for their use. There are variations in peg designs, shapes, and materials that provide different sounds when used on a given surface. Surfaces other than slate are also used. Quartz, marble, and several aluminum alloys are made into friction calls. Some alloys provide sound almost identical to slate, but have the advantage of being unbreakable and easier to maintain. There are several types of grooved calls utilizing aluminum alloys. These provide neophytes with a guided surface on which to make their calls. This eliminates many potential mistakes, but restricts the sounds possible to the user. Again these, like all of the above, will not produce a gobble and require two hands to operate.

There are several push-button or crank-operated calls where the striker is held against the plate within a sound box by some means that predetermines its movement, like the grooved callers but even more limiting. They provide beginners with acceptable sounds almost automatically, but greatly limit the variety of sounds possible. Some of these can be operated using only one hand.

Two of the easiest calls to operate, especially for novices, are the grooved type (left) and the push-button call.

Suction calls are another of the many available devices. Several kinds of suction calls are on the market.

Most friction calls are rendered inoperable or limited when wet, a difficulty not encountered with mouth calls.

Among mouth or air-operated calls, suction calls, which are variations of the old wingbone call, may date back farther than any other type. Sound is produced by drawing air through a tube or orifice. Some find these calls difficult to use. But when mastered they produce a distinctive tone which sounds particularly true at a distance.

Adult hen turkey wingbones are usually best for suction type calls. Either two or three wingbones, inserted progressively into each other so the smallest one provides the mouth piece orifice and the largest the bell or sound chamber, are used. Many variations of this call have been made, including one named after Tom Turpin which is a wooden copy with a hard rubber mouthpiece. The Johenning box must be included here, but in its case the air is drawn over a diaphragm rather than through an orifice.

It is more difficult to master a variety of sounds with a suction call than with other air-operated calls. Once mastered, though, they provide exceptionally true sound.

I have yet, however, to hear an acceptable gobble made with one of these calls. Also, though they may be operated while holding them in the mouth with one hand, the other hand is needed to vary the emitted sound.

Tube calls and snuff cans are blown outside the mouth. Expelled air, traveling over a diaphragm, produces the sound which can be varied by changes in air pressure; changes in position of lip or tongue on the diaphragm; changes in the configuration of the operators mouth; and, in the case of one patented type of tube, mechanically through the use of an internal plunger. This versatility of sound production is the reason why these calls are so popular in the calling of all game, including elk, geese, predators, and turkey. One type call, in the hands of a practiced caller, can imitate the call of all these animals.

The tube call, being an external mouth call, means anyone can use it with practice. It is capable of both loud (and for many, probably the longest range type of call in production) and very soft sounds. All turkey talk can be made on it including nearly perfect gobbles. But, like all calls listed previously, it requires at least one hand to operate. Another disadvantage of most tubes is the diaphragm material which deteriorates, and when replaced it requires adjustment and therefore is difficult for beginners to handle. Some are available with preset diaphragms.

Yet another calling device is the tube call. Most such calls have cords or lanyards attached so they can be hung from the hunter's neck where they can be reached and used quickly.

Mouth, or diaphragm, calls are widely used because they produce an excellent sound and leave both hands free. Having the hands free while using a call can be a big advantage when luring a tom into range. However, some hunters find mouth calls difficult to master.

Mouth diaphragms are held inside the mouth against the palate or upper part of the mouth. The sound is controlled by the tongue's placement on the diaphragm and the configuration of the mouth as well as air pressure. Diaphragms are made in a variety of thicknesses and are held within a containing yoke. Because of this variety, both loud and soft sounds can be made as can all turkey sounds including the gobble. However, the gobble and some other sounds are somewhat more difficult to produce.

The great advantage of a mouth-held diaphragm is that it leaves both hands free. Unfortunately, not everyone can use a mouth-held diaphragm. Some with dental work, odd palate shape, or gagging problems cannot use this call. And for the rest of us it is probably the most difficult to get used to or to learn to operate well.

Mouth-held diaphragm calls are popular in calling contests as most contestants are highly skilled and spend many hours practicing. They are sometimes made with two, three, or more layers of diaphragm material. This allows the skilled caller limitless sounds, including some so raspy it is hard to distinguish them from a good friction call. One problem, however, is, that after use, multiple diaphragms tend to stick together and unless you are very careful you will find your favorite call not performing when you want it. (The Penn's Woods "Spacer" diaphragm is largely free of this problem.)

It is a good idea after you use your multiple diaphragm mouth call to insert pieces of toothpick, pine needle, or leaf stem, between the diaphragms before putting it away.

One last type of diaphragm call is bellows-operated. These are basically limited, although not entirely, to making the gobble and are widely used for locating turkeys as will be discussed in later chapters.

Most diaphragms are made of latex which deteriorates in heat or ultra violet light. Longevity can be improved by storing in a cool, dark place. This is not necessary with those made of silicone rubber.

Here's what Bart Jacob had to say about calling in one of his magazine articles (March-April, 1981 issue of *Turkey Call*):

The big wild turkey was in plain view through the open hardwoods, though still more than 100 yards away. He was a magnificent tom, and he was showing off after every few steps. From my position in a recent blow-down, I watched his approach through the "V" formed by two trees a dozen feet in front of me. It was like looking through the notch of a rifle

Bellows, or shaker, calls are used for gobbling and are often favored as locator calls.

sight. His line of travel never strayed. He came straight as an arrow for the hen he heard me imitate on my box call.

He would gobble and display, then take a few more steps, make two gobbles, and then another display. My fingers shook and my heart pounded. Finally, at about 30 yards, he disappeared behind one of the two trees in front of me. When he reappeared on the other side, I took him.

Standing over this beautiful 20-pound trophy, my companions remarked on just how classic the hunt had been. Was it good calling that made it so? The hunt had been recorded on tape by an outdoor writer, who, with a wildlife artist and a hunting companion, had been hiding behind me.

The tape would be the basis of a good story. When we played it back, all the sounds of the early morning woods, the gobbling of the turkey, and our spontaneous shouts and comments after the shot were marvelous and amusing to hear. But the calling—I couldn't believe it—was terrible. I know how to use a box call. I had used it successfully more than once. Most recently for my hunting companion just the day before. What had happened?

I played the tape over and over, and I still couldn't understand how a wild turkey could be fooled by those sounds. Apparently, like the guy who can break every clay pigeon he shoots at on the range, but misses most of the ducks on the bay, in my excitement I hadn't been able to do anything right. I was lucky, though, because this turkey was "hot," and I had the feeling that if I was a squeaking tree he would have probably still come in and then, finding no hen, would have walked off in a huff.

Turkeys are like that. Many more times than most hunters realize, spring or fall, old birds or young, turkeys will come to "poor" calls. And they will sometimes come to calls so easily and quickly that the hunter can be caught off guard.

One early fall morning, I succeeded in breaking up a large flock of young birds. I located my hunting companion, as it was his turn for a shot, and we sat down on either side of a big pine tree at the flush site. It was at the edge of an overgrown pasture with patches of low-lying juniper and scattered pines.

I blew one "kee-kee run" on my tube, and got an immediate response from a bird about 100 yards in front of me. I elbowed my partner and blew a second "kee-kee." Again the answer came almost before I had finished, this time from half the distance. I urged my partner to turn in my direction and get ready, as this bird was obviously coming in fast. With my third call, a head popped up over a juniper at about 20 yards and a nice young jake was added to the turkey report.

Of course, it isn't always that way, but turkeys can be fooled with little effort when they are so inclined.

I have a friend who was hunting fall turkeys by himself one morning. (He usually hunts with me and I do the calling.) He sat down in a good spot where turkeys had been entering a corn field, hoping to be lucky enough to get a shot. Then, off to his right he thought he heard a gobble, which he immediately pegged as an inexperienced hunter who didn't know turkeys don't gobble in the fall.

When he heard the gobble again, and this time it sounded like more than one, he realized it was the real thing. Not eager to try calling, but left with few choices, he thought, "Well, if they are gobbling, I had better give them a couple of those hen yelps on my box, just like in the spring." A couple of yelps produced an immediate reaction: two jakes approached, sounding off with yelps and short gobbles.

My friend was amazed. First of all, he never tried calling a turkey before; and secondly, what he was doing seemed to be all wrong for this time of year—but, it was working. After a few more exchanges of this turkey talk he was able to shoot a nice 14-pound, 2-inch-bearded jake.

When he arrived at my place to show off the bird, his eyes were filled with tears of joy and excitement. But when he demonstrated what he did, I pointed out the coarseness of the hen side of his box caller. The jakes weren't coming in to a sexy little hen; rather, they thought they were coming to join an old long-lost drinking buddy, another jake. But it worked. And if my friend hadn't tried, he would still be relying on others to call in his birds.

There are a lot of new turkey hunters who could share that turkey hunter's experience if they would go out on their own and try. Their calling might not sound good at all, but it might be just good enough for a particular turkey. Many experts tend to make too much of calling expertise, and nobody can blame them, because it is only natural to tout the thing you do best. But such an attitude can discourage the average potential turkey hunter.

There are, of course, many times when turkeys don't react like this at all, when they won't even come to the caller no matter how good he is. But then again, the answer seems to be in trying—only this time in trying something different.

Last spring, in Vermont, I was sitting well hidden on the side of a knoll yelping at a gobbler across a small ravine in which a brook was tumbling down the mountainside. The gobbler climbed the mountain, crossed the brook, and came back down my side. But with him were two hens. As he descended on my side within sight, but out of range, I continued giving him soft hen yelps, to which he would gobble in answer. My excitement rose—and then fell as he just kept on going by me on down the brook. I tried my sexiest yelps and most exciting cackles, but he continued on with his two hens.

In desperation I made a loud flat cluck on my "Imitator" call, and, to my surprise, one of the hens turned back and started up the knoll toward me, clucking continuously as she came. The second hen and tom followed.

The first hen was now within 10 feet, and the second was walking directly in front of the Tom, preventing a shot. Talk about a case of uncontrolled nervous shaking—now the first hen was out of my vision, behind me, still clucking. Finally, the second hen stepped out of the way so I could shoot my gobbler, just six measured paces from where I sat. The one cluck had changed the hunt.

Later that spring, I had a chance to try it again in New York State. I worked a gobbler all morning, and he would travel back and forth along the edge of a field, sounding off all the time but refusing to come to where I was in the woods.

I changed positions several times, and tried to get closer, to intercept him, but to no avail. Finally, he crossed through a small draw to a knoll on the other side of the field and continued gobbling. When he sounded like he was on the far side of the knoll, I crept across the field and was about to crawl through a barbed wire fence on the other side when I heard him coming back. I hid as best I could, next to an old apple tree on the fence line and, having yelped at him all morning without success, decided to try my cluck. One cluck and he was running toward me. At first, he was partially screened by a tangle of wild grape vines, then he burst out into the open 30 feet away.

Twice the cluck turned the trick. Yet, many experts will tell you never to use it as it might sound like the alarm putt. I'm awfully glad I tried.

Probably the most interesting experience I have had in trying to fool a turkey took place on a fall hunt in New York. My hunting partner and I headed up either side of a ridge to look for turkeys. I heard a shot from his direction and rushed to join him. He explained that just as he came into view of a cornfield, he saw turkeys running into the woods, and got off a shot, hoping it would scatter the birds. The turkeys were barely out of sight when he fired, so he was unsure whether they had flown or not. So we decided to split up and continue in that direction, keeping in touch with our box calls until we could determine if there were any lonely birds around.

Just after getting back together, we heard a jake yelp and "kee-kee" below us, across a ravine. We sat down under a pine top, my partner covering the approach to the left while I covered the right. After some turkey conversation, me with a mouth yelper, the jake flew across the ravine and landed at the edge of the woods above and to my right. My partner had not seen this and was surprised to see me swivel around to cover that direction. However, when the jake answered my next call, my pal realized what had happened.

For almost an hour the turkey and I kept up a regular chit-chat. The jake would sneak back and forth, first near and then far, but always answering. I tried shutting up for a while, but this seemed to drive him away. I even tried answering his occasional short gobbles with some of my own, which were far from good but didn't have any effect, good or bad, on the turkey. His basic language was the "kee-kee run," and after a while, when I compared it to mine, the more I realized that while my whistle, or "kee-kee," sounded like his, my following yelps were not as deep and coarse as his. Feeling this might be bothering him, I tried the "kee-kee" alone. He still would come and go, but never get within range. He was a smart one, and it just wasn't to his satisfaction.

Finally, as I could just make him out standing on the hill behind us, I had an idea. I made the "kee-kee run" by whistling the "kee-kee" on my mouth yelper, followed with two yelps on the coarse side of my box. The jake stepped right out. Where before he had paced silently, now he noisily marched down through the leaves right for us. It reminded me of how a big spring bird stamps along toward you when he decides you are a real hen.

My partner got his gun on the jake as he stepped behind a tree, and his march was stopped by the following shot.

The combination I used triggered that certain something in the turkey's brain making everything right for him. The hunt was one of my most memorable, and I'm glad I tried one more sound one more time, and it worked.

Calling doesn't always have to be good to work; and even if it is always good, it doesn't always work. But as a fisherman friend of mine loves to say, "You can't catch a salmon unless your fly is in the water," and you can't call a turkey to your gun unless you try calling. With the right combination and a little luck, you will have accomplished, bar none, the greatest thrill of all hunting.

Chapter 6

PRIMARY EQUIPMENT: Guns, Bows & Cameras

Shotguns

The single shot, exposed hammer, shotgun has killed many turkeys. More importantly, it is often the most inexpensive, practical gun for the young, new turkey hunter. It forces hunters to make the first shot count.

But ever since repeaters were invented, we have taken advantage of extra shots. When the first shot hasn't quite done the job—and a turkey can absorb a tremendous amount—it is both practical and humane to be able to follow it up immediately. For this reason the double barrel has its advantage over the single shot. The two converging barrels of a side-by-side often have different impact points and when you are shooting tight groups at close range this can cause a miss. A side-by-side must be patterned so you can compensate for this. Most over-and-unders do not have this problem because they are usually manufactured with parallel, rather than converging, barrels.

Side-by-sides and over-and-unders, however, often have the two barrels choked differently. Ideally, you should use a full choke barrelled gun. If your gun is equipped with a modified and full choke barrel you may have to lure your gobbler in closer in order to use the modified barrel first.

In the many areas where the shotgun is used for turkey hunting, a relatively small contingent of sportsmen swear by the 10-gauge as the surest way to anchor a bird. Shown here are side-by-side and single-barrel models.

Therefore, the best type of shotgun is the repeater, of which there are several types: bolt actions, which are slow and cumbersome to operate, but very dependable; pump actions which are the favorite of many and

Ammunition commonly used to hunt wild turkeys includes the 12-gauge short buffered magnum at left, the 12-gauge 3-inch buffered magnum at center and the 10-gauge 3½-inch magnum at right.

are fast, simple, and dependable to operate, but have a lot of action noise except in the hands of an expert, and finally the autoloader, both recoil and gas operated. The autoloader has a fast action and the action noise is hidden in the sound of the shot. If the autoloader has one drawback, it is that the action sometimes jams.

A little more here on pump-action noise. First of all, if you are hunting in an area where you may kill more than one turkey in a given day and you have downed one bird the noise of the shot sometimes does not scare other birds. They are more interested in why the shot bird is behaving so strangely. But if you have to work the action (unless you have great experience with a pump) for the second shot, they will hear it and be on their way. A pump also requires more movement on your part to work the action than an autoloader does. Additionally, unless a pump action is fully closed, it rattles and clanks while being carried.

One morning I picked up two gun industry representatives I was guiding after roosting a good old tom the night before. Carrying two new model pumps and being very safety minded, they struggled up the hill with actions open and empty. The old bird kept gobbling from the roost as the clatter continued toward him. Once we set-up and they

Typical aiming equipment for turkey hunting with a shotgun includes (from top) open sights, double bead, and optical sight.

loaded-up, I let things quiet down for awhile, hoping the gobbler would forget all about it. After a while I made a cluck or two and he responded as if nothing had happened, but when fly-down time came, he hit the ground running in the opposite direction just as fast as he could go. This could happen for many other reasons, but I believe the sound of the actions scared the bird.

The shotgun, regardless of type, will only do the job if the gauge, choke, and load are right. First, the gauge should be large enough to handle the heaviest load you can comfortably shoot. I recommend 12 gauge and preferably one with 3-inch chambers. With the right choke and loads, this will kill a turkey out to 40 yards.

If you refuse to shoot over 20 yards, you can get away with a 16 or 20 gauge. But, don't assume by going to a 10 gauge you can shoot a turkey at 60 to 80 yards. You can, of course, shoot at one at that distance and be lucky enough to kill it, but remember the adage "pattern goes before penetration is lost." If you keep your shots under 40 yards (and if you called the turkey in that far you've had the satisfaction of doing it right) you may have an advantage in killing ability with a 3½-inch 10 gauge over the 12 gauge, but you took an unnecessary bruising. The modern, big 10 is meant for knocking down high passing geese that do not run away after coming down with a broken wing.

The choke should be full to give the tightest possible pattern. Be aware that you are shooting at a turkey's head which is smaller than your fist. If your favorite gun has only a modified choke you can compensate somewhat by using a buffered load, but you would be better advised to insist on a closer shot.

While discussing choke, let us discuss barrel length. Back in slow burning, black powder days a longer barrel meant a more efficient burn

Camouflage is a very important aid, and many turkey hunters have borrowed a waterfowling tactic by camouflaging even their guns. Several kinds of tapes and paints are shown. Most hunters prefer a sleeve or tape that can be easily removed form a gun.

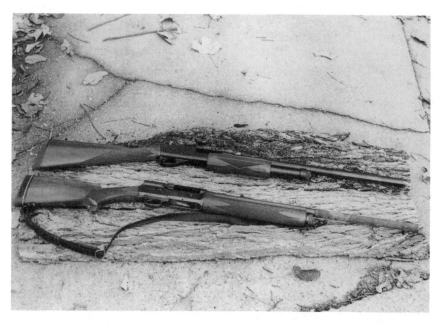

Short-barreled guns are popular for hunting in woodlands, as they handle easily and quickly in relatively tight quarters. The guns shown here are a Remington (top) and Bart Jacob's short-barreled Browning.

and increased velocity or range. Goose guns have carried the long barrel tradition into modern cartridge times. They have long barrels because goose hunters can use a longer sighting plane and added barrel weight for good swing and follow-through. With modern powders, barrel length, until it's almost illegally short, has very little effect on range and no effect on pattern size or density. Range is a factor of load, and pattern a factor of choke and load. If you have a choice use the shortest, full-choked, barrel available. This will save you a lot of grief when carrying your gun, particularly if slung over your shoulder, and it makes a big difference in getting your gun on target in cramped quarters.

Extensive testing by manufacturers proved that modern powders burn completely in the first 18-20 inches of the barrel. In a few cases added barrel length reduced velocity due to friction of wad and shot column against the inside of the barrel. Therefore a 22-inch full choked barrel shot in some tests with greater velocity than a 32-inch full choked barrel with the same load.

Remington has been a leader in the production of short, full-choke, barrel shotguns. In their tests, barrel length had little, if any, effect on velocity.

A turkey must be hit in the head or neck to ensure an "on the spot" kill. A turkey hit in the lung or some other vital spot will also be a kill, but it will seldom be an "on the spot" kill and this is as important as it is unique. Any other big game animal, and in most states turkeys are considered big game, when vitally hit will run or walk a short distance and die, usually leaving a blood trail and signs of where it went. This may be followed up by the hunter and the animal is collected. A turkey has the same capability of leaving the scene when vitally hit. To me, it seems to have this capability to an extreme. Unfortunately, unlike other animals, it doesn't leave a blood trail because its feathers absorb the blood. Rarely, does it leave a scuffed up trail on the ground. Rather, with the exception of a few feathers in and around the place of impact, it is usually off and soaring on fixed wings, until it collapses in flight. Unless the hunter hears or sees the turkey fall, it is lost and wasted except to feed a turkey predator.

The only sure way to anchor a turkey is to hit him with enough shot in the head and neck so that, except for the usual flopping, he goes nowhere. To do this, the shot pattern must be tight enough to carry

In this photo, Ben Conger demonstrates the convenience of a short-barreled gun in the woods.

With his short-barreled gun, Bart Jacob moves easily under a limb. A sling isn't necessary but can leave a hand free when you're carrying a bird and also can stabilize the shooting arm when drawing a bead on a gobbler.

sufficient shot to the target. Since heavier shot has greater penetration, buy the heaviest shot that will, in your particular gun give a pattern tight or dense enough to put enough pellets in this fist sized area at a given maximum yardage. My gun puts 15-20 No. 4 shot in the head and neck area at 40 yards. My son's slide-action requires No. 6 shot to do the same thing.

Some hunters swear by No. 2 shot. But I have yet to see a barrel that will place enough No. 2 shot in a pattern as described above for me to recommend it. These hunters, who swear by No. 2 shot because it has such great weight, therefore penetration, claim you can miss the head and kill the turkey with a body shot (and you know how I feel about this). Remember, "pattern goes before penetration is lost." Since deep penetration is not required in head and neck shots, due to the high vulnerability here, pattern is the most important consideration.

Number 2 shot has its place, however, and I use it as a follow up. I use two No. 4s then a No. 2 in my Browning, for a bird that has been crippled and is trying to get away. Only when trying to kill a cripple should one take anything but a head shot. Number 2 shot does wonders on geese but geese come down with a broken wing and cannot escape on foot—not so with turkeys.

Getting to the loads, we have magnums both 2¾-inch and 3-inch (and 10 gauge 3½-inch) and new buffered plated loads made by all three major American manufacturers. I take advantage of all of this because in turkey hunting a box of shells goes a long way. A three-inch magnum stuffs more shot and powder into the cartridge. And the shot will fly truer and in a tighter pattern when buffered with plastic powder which fills the voids between the packed shot, and copper plating which hardens the shot, so it deforms less when passing through the choke. If you shoot only when the turkey is within 20 feet these tight shooting, buffered loads are a disadvantage as they only open up about as big as a tennis ball at that range and you would be better off with standard high base shells.

The potential of very close shots brings up the use of sights or sighting arrangements. As just mentioned, the pattern of any shell is tighter and smaller, depending on the load and choke, the closer one gets to the target. At very close range it's almost like shooting a single projectile

Here's another popular gun, the pump-action Mossberg Model 500 Turkey gun.

which normally requires a sight of some kind. Additionally, a turkey hunter is often in an abnormal, cramped, and strained position when shooting. He also has a tendency to be watching the old gobbler strut his stuff and to be mentally measuring his beard over the end of his shotgun barrel when he fires. For all of these reasons, it is advantageous to use a simple sight of some kind or a sighting arrangement that forces him to be on target when he shoots.

The simplest of these is the rib. If you have one on your barrel install a second smaller bead halfway down the rib. By lining up the smaller bead behind the front bead you have a sighting arrangement. There are optical shotgun sights on the market, all of which are very effective. On some a bright red dot is seen only when the gun is properly cheeked and lined up and the dot can be adjusted to the point of impact. The simplest of these is the Accu-Sight.

The ultimate in shotgun sights is the fully adjustable open sight found on barrels sold for deer hunting with slugs.

Camouflage is another necessity for the serious hunter, and to some extent his firearm. It is a shame to paint a classic shotgun, but some do. For them there are "camo" paints, the kind that are easily removed with common solvents and the peel-off vinyls.

For those who are not willing to paint their guns, there are "camo" tapes available which you can put around the entire gun or just the barrel (this is all I camouflage). These tapes come in several materials. Some vinyl tapes work well, but others show white when the color is scratched off. The best of these tapes is made of fabric, but it is hard to find. All tapes should be removed after the season so rust does not have a chance to develop underneath.

There are also covers in "camo" naughehyde material that are customized to fit a particular model gun. Full camouflage on a gun gives a hunter confidence and he can at least say it wasn't his gun that spooked the turkey, but be careful when you lay your gun down in the leaves—you may never see it again.

Another practical thing on a turkey gun is a carrying sling. This can be an add-on, or permanent type, and swivels are available to make it part of the gun. Watch out for shiny hardware. A detachable sling with a lace tied through the loops at either end can also double as a turkey tote.

I consider my own gun to be nearly ideal for turkey. I use a humpback, recoil-operated Browning Auto 5 in 12 gauge, 3-inch magnum. When I bought it I got several barrels, including a 24-inch slug barrel with ramp

Bart Jacob sets up a pattern sheet to test his gun before setting out on a hunt. This is an excellent idea, and more hunters should take the time to do it. Knowing how your gun shoots with given loads at various distances can make the difference between coming home with a turkey dinner and coming home skunked.

front sight and fully adjustable open rear sight. With this barrel came a knurled magazine cap with sling swivel attachment. I sent this barrel away and had a screw-in, extra full-choke tube installed. I have a tube of the original bore to replace this if I ever want the barrel for its original intended use. This gives me a short (24-inch) full-choked barrel with an adjustable sight.

Next I removed (no easy task) the shiny, plastic-like finish from both the butt stock and fore-end. I refinished the wood with a dull, hand-rubbed finish. Now it looks perfectly natural in a woodland setting. I covered the barrel with a good fabric "camo" tape held back from the fore-end just enough to allow free recoil operation.

When my gun is in my lap or over my knee the receiver is hidden in my gloved hand. At other times the only thing the turkey sees is the "O" of the muzzle.

Last, I shortened the butt stock by a half-inch and squared off the toe angle so it is not as sharp, and added hardware for a detachable sling. The shorter buttstock allows me to get the gun up in spite of a near prone position and also helps when I am waterfowl hunting with a heavy jacket. The "softer" toe helps when you are shooting in an awkward position, hard left off your biceps, or hard right (if you are right handed) off your chest. The sling attachment allows for its use and is not in the way at other times. In my opinion, the tool is nearly perfect. The only real potential fault is in the user.

Two major gun manufacturers now produce short barrelled, full-choked guns for turkey hunters. For the hunter who prefers a lighter, more maneuverable gun, Remington has introduced its Model 1100 Special Field in 12 gauge with a 21-inch barrel, full choke and 2¾-inch chamber (buffered magnum loads available). This gun has a ventilated rib, straight stock, and weighs only 7¼ pounds. Remington has also come out with a full-choked 21-inch barrel option for their Model 870 slide-action with 3-inch chambers, it is known as the 870 Special Field. This gun is also equipped with a straight stock, ventilated rib, and double-bead sighting.

For the hunter who will not settle for less than the most firepower available, Ithaca Gun Co. has come out with a turkey hunter's version of its gas operated Mag-10. This gun is equipped with a 26-inch full choke, ventilated rib, barrel, and nylon web padded sling with quick detach swivels. It has a matte-blue finish and tung oiled stock and fore-end. It also comes with a double-bead sighting arrangement.

A third manufacturer, Mossberg, has introduced a turkey hunter's version of its Model 500, 12 gauge, slide action. It is equipped with a ventilated rib 20-inch barrel with interchangeable choke tubes including a full choke. It is also equipped with sling swivels and a camo web sling.

No matter what you use, sighting-in and patterning are a must. Remember, two barrels of the same choke do not shoot the same and a side-by-side can have two different impact points. There are some good pattern sheets on the market that have a life-size silhouette of a turkey's head and neck. The better sheets have an aiming point at the base of his warty head. You are not interested in how many pellets are in a 30-inch circle, but how many are in the head and neck at the yardage you expect to shoot. To get more shot in this vital area you must use one or more of the following: a tighter choke, a larger gauge, a smaller shot size, a heavier buffered load, or fire at a closer range. Above all when the time comes, sight carefully and make the first shot count.

Archery Equipment

There is a growing number of archers today either going back to, or just plain hooked, on instinctive shooting with a long bow or working recurve. They are purists. They trade off some of the advantages of technology for the sheer beauty and challenge of their equipment.

This challenge is probably brought to its highest degree when involved with hunting the wild turkey gobbler. The instinctive shooter with a long-bow has to not only know his own abilities but he has to allow for the awkward length of his bow, its relative lack of speed and the need to draw and shoot all in one motion. The working recurve has the advantage over the long-bow in being shorter and easier to draw from a sitting or kneeling position and being slightly faster in arrow speed. In either case, skill acquired from constant practice is as important as any other skill to a turkey hunter.

Those who cannot spend great amounts of time practicing or who wish to take advantage of modern technology should use the compound bow. With the compound a hunter has a reasonable chance at taking a gobbler. A compound bow is relatively compact and can be held upright from a kneeling and certain sitting positions. It has good arrow speed and most important, because of its "let off" it is capable of being comfortably held for a limited amount of time in the full draw position. This gives the hunter the advantage of taking the time to use an accurate set of sights and the advantage of drawing when the turkey cannot see the motion and holding until the turkey is in the open.

Although the traditional longbow and recurve bow are slowly regaining popularity, it's the compound bow—as illustrated here—that is most often taken afield by turkey-hunting archers.

One of the disadvantages of the compound is that if you hold it upright and ready with the end resting on the ground while waiting for the shot the wheel or cam can get loaded with dirt and other debris and a cable may be thrown. The same can happen if debris is caught under the cable when carrying it through the woods. New cam bows are more susceptible to this, but they also add greater arrow speed. I personally like my light two-wheel with recurved limbs the best for this type of hunting.

Though you can rest the end of your bow on the ground while waiting for your gobbler to appear, never try unleashing an arrow with a bow limb close to, or touching, the ground. When the string of a bow is released the tips of the bow arms actually move farther away from the center of the bow handle. If an arrow is unleashed with the end of one limb hitting the ground, the arrow will be cast violently upward as the limbs flex. While practicing your shooting, try unleashing an arrow with one limb touching the ground and you will always remember this no-no.

An internal cam bow that probably represents one of the highest states of technology today is the Oneida Eagle made by Oneida Labs. This bow combines great arrow speed with exceptionally quiet, smooth operation. It also has conventional limb tips so no cable, wheels, or cams can get in the mud when rested on the ground.

The shooting weight for a turkey bow should be the one you are most comfortable with, particularly when holding it at full draw—50 pounds is fine. Of course, if you are used to a heavier bow, all the better because this will increase arrow speed. At 20 yards or more a turkey can jump or duck

Hunting heads for turkeys include (from left) the Bear with turkey stopper, the Viper (closed and open), and the Anderson with Scorpio.

an arrow with amazing ease. I believe they do this on sight rather than due to bow or string sound. Therefore arrow speed is an important factor.

The purist will use cedar arrows, fletched with wild turkey feathers. The rest of us should use the lightest, good grade aluminum arrow with a dull green, brown or "camo" finish, that matches our bow weight in spine and our draw in length. Penetration is not a problem so arrow weight should be sacrificed for speed. The most practical, all-weather fletching is plastic. The plastic vanes should be in dull greens and browns, a fluorescent bright colored nock can help in watching arrow flight and in retrieval and will not be seen by the turkey.

The arrow is not complete without the head and there is yet to be developed a perfect arrow head for hunting turkeys.

The most popular arrangement is any good quality broadhead attached to the shaft over a "turkey stopper." This is a multi-bladed unit with dull edges that serves to slow down the arrow after the head has penetrated, providing greater shock and tissue damage. Some use a flat washer mounted in the same position to do this job. The problem is that you can successfully skewer a gobbler and he can fly or run off with the skewer. My present personal choice is a head called the "Viper." It comes in three or four-blade models which open up on impact. Flight feather, tissue, and bone damage are maximized with this head.

A new turkey arrow concept that looks promising, but that I have yet to field test is the use of the Zwickey Scorpio with a large head like the Anderson Magnum. The Scorpio mounted behind the head actually slides up the shaft as the head penetrates. The fit is tight enough to create drag, dissipating the entire shock of the hit into the animal, while preventing the arrow from passing through. Therefore, the arrow stops in the turkey.

Perhaps the most important thing in anchoring your gobbler with an arrow is impact point. The point to hit is the wing butt when the turkey is sideways to you and dead center of the upper body mass when he is facing toward you or directly away. In any case we are talking about an extremely small target, particularly when compared to the chest cavity of a deer or elk. For this reason, a good set of sights is important. Notice, I said "set" of sights. Our natural anchor point (the rear sight for an archer is controlled by the anchor point) may not seem natural when kneeling or sitting, therefore a front and rear sight combination is more accurate than just a set of pins. There are quite a few options available from string peeps to more sophisticated sighting arrangements which include the same type of optical sights as are available for shotguns.

Modern quivers are part of the bow. This has advantages and disadvantages. A bow quiver puts those arrows right where you need them, and when traveling through brush you only have to maneuver the bow in your hand. However, the bow quiver and arrows double the mass you are holding in front of the turkey. And if the arrows are brightly fletched it is like waving a flag at him. For this reason I use a quick-detachable quiver. Lots of them say "quick-detachable" but require a lot of effort with a tendency to create noise when detaching. But some are quick and quiet, and often the others with a little work will do the same. I detach my quiver as soon as I set-up on the turkey and have nocked my arrow. I then lay the quiver and the rest of my arrows on the ground where they are handy, but out of sight. This not only reduces the visual mass of my bow, but makes it lighter in my hand and provides a greater field of vision for me as I hold it ready for the shot.

The "ready to shoot position" of a bow still presents far more for the turkey to see than the muzzle of a shotgun and full camouflage is a must.

I painted my bow with removable spray-on paint made for this purpose rather than using the vinyl peel-off paint because I spray everything—wheels, fittings, the works.

The most important thing is to eliminate any possible shine or glare. The rest of it is up to the artistic talents of the hunter. Bold patterns in "camo" colors that wrap around the edges of the bow handle and limbs can do a terrific job of obscuring the bow. "Camo" bow tape, the same kind as used on shotguns, can be used if you don't want to paint your bow, but it is only effective on the limbs. "Camo" fabric sleeves are also available for the limbs but when wet they get heavy and affect bow performance.

Other accessories which can be useful, depending on the archer's personal preferences, are cable guards, arrow rests, arrow releases, and stabilizers. Stabilizers can help in accurate shooting, but, like all accessories, they should be camouflaged.

Two additional products should be mentioned. First, the several makes of string trackers which when attached to the bow with the free running string tied to the arrow provide another way of tracking and retrieving a hit bird. The benefits of this may be slightly offset by the tendency to slow down the arrow's flight except at very close range. The other is a simple wire-form clip that when attached to the bow will accommodate a small leafy or needled branch which can further hide the bow from the sharp eyes of the turkey and instills confidence in the hunter as he peeks through the leaves over his arrow at the turkey. This unit is called the "Outline-Breaker."

My own bow, as I mentioned earlier, is a light two-wheeler with recurved limbs, a Talon MK3 made by Golden Eagle. It is adjustable from 50-to-70 pounds pull. I shoot it at 50 pounds for turkeys and crank it up to 65 pounds for deer and elk. It has a full 50 percent let-off. It is completely painted in camo colors and is equipped with an Altier sight using an optical Accu-Sight span. It is also equipped with an Outline-Breaker and a quick detachable "camo" painted quiver. I shoot 2114 Gamegetters with brown plastic vanes and Viper broadheads. It is all I want and need in a turkey bow.

Sights, depending on type, should be set in the 20-to-30 yard range. Practice should be done with field points matching the weight of your broadheads. However, prior to the season it is important to try the broadheads as even if the weight is the same, some will fly differently. An

Camera gear ranges from the sophisticated (and expensive) rig at top to the easy-to-use 35mm pocket model at bottom. Pocket cameras are easily toted on a hunt and they'll do nicely for post-hunt shots of a sportsman and his trophy.

Using the Orvis tiny tripod and a camera equipped with a self-timer and cable release, a hunter can photograph himself.

inexpensive Etha-Foam target is best for practice and will not harm the broadheads, but chops up quickly. Practice shooting at the smallest impact point possible so when the time comes to shoot that turkey you don't end up with just a pile of neatly cut-off feathers good only for tying trout flies.

Photography

Photography for serious photographers will be discussed later in a separate chapter. What we are concerned with here is the average turkey hunter wanting to record his hunt and its success or failure.

The first consideration in any camera is its weight. I have a 35mm camera with a telephoto lens that weighs in at 13 pounds. It takes fantastic photographs. However, when I go gobbler hunting my basic gear consists of: gun, decoy, calls, extra shells, insulated seat, vacuum bottle of coffee and a sandwich, all of which weigh in at just over 20 pounds. The 13 pounds of camera brings my total up to 33 pounds. Now if I make the mistake of shooting a 20-pound gobbler I'm coming out of the woods carrying 50-plus pounds. Obviously, the thing to do is not shoot a gobbler, but if I don't shoot a gobbler why did I carry all that gear into the woods?

To be of any value a hunter's camera must be light. If it weighs much more than an additional turkey call, leave it in camp and carry the turkey call. Also, it must be small, not necessarily diminutive, but certainly small enough to fit in a pocket or your daypack and not take up any more room than a good box call, less if possible.

A hunter's camera must also be super-simple to operate. Preferably, it should be a camera with which you are very familiar. If you have to take out a manual and spend several minutes reading before you can figure out what buttons to push, you are going to get disgusted and leave the camera home, in camp, or on the front seat of your vehicle. The camera you use to take photographs of the kids, your dog, or even your grand-children, is the one to take turkey hunting with you. You are familiar with it and its working has become almost second nature to you. You won't need to take a "crash course" in photography every time you want to take a photograph.

As a hunter you are interested in showing the steps of your hunt and the ultimate picture, which is you with your trophy.

As a rule, if you have eight to twelve photographs of you preparing for the hunt and actually hunting prior to the kill you have enough. One good shot of you at the time of your harvesting the bird—this will probably have to be a reenactment—and perhaps three to four shots of you after the kill is enough to tell the entire story of your hunt without becoming boring.

As mentioned, the camera to take with you should be the one with which you are familiar. It makes no difference if it is a new disc type, an instant film type, or even a miniature 35mm (which is what I carry), as long as it is light enough so you won't leave it home and easy enough to operate so you can take a picture without taking a photography course.

Besides being lightweight and easy to operate, there is a third feature the camera you choose to carry while hunting should have: it should either have a built-in self-timer or be able to be fitted with a self-timing device. Turkey hunting is not done in a crowd. When you get your gobbler you are almost surely going to be alone in the woods. And unless you have a self-timer on your camera or are a contortionist it is going to be extremely difficult to take a picture from behind the camera of yourself and your gobbler out in front of the camera. There are many devices on the market such as extra long shutter-operating cables, and even radio-operated shutter releases, but most of them are too heavy and get you right back into the heavyweight camera syndrome. A camera with a self-timer in it, or a simple self-timer accessory, is the answer if you want a picture of yourself and your turkey.

The only other thing needed is a way to steady your camera while you race back to kneel or stand near your turkey waiting for the self-timer to activate the shutter.

Usually, you can set your camera on a rock or log, but one of the tiny, portable tripods is better. Another good trick is to rest your camera on a sandbag such as used for supporting rifles when bench rest shooting. Lacking any of these you would be surprised how steady a glove or sock filled with dirt is. And if you stick one foot behind the other no one who views your photographs will ever notice you are missing one sock.

If all cameras have one common enemy it is moisture. A few minutes in the rain or the same amount of time in the breast pocket of a hunter who is perspiring heavily during an uphill climb (I lost one camera lens mechanism due to this) is all it takes to render a camera a total loss. There are several solutions to this problem, but most either make the camera difficult to carry or place it in a location where it is difficult to get to when you want it. The best solution I have come up with so far is to place it in a plastic zip-lock bag before putting it in a pocket. The bag also keeps out dirt.

Chapter 7

OTHER EQUIPMENT

We talked about turkey calls used to entice that old gobbler in the spring and the equipment used to harvest him whether by shot, arrow, or on film. What other equipment is needed?

The first thing to come to mind is camouflage. We have already talked about the birds' keen eyesight, its lack of curiosity, and how seeing a strange object simply causes a bird to vanish. However, if we sit still and wear full camouflage that blends into our surroundings we can remain unobserved without hiding behind or in something. It is obvious that we need clothing suitable to the temperature and weather conditions of the location and the season. Often in spring in northern climates it will be frosty and chilly before the sun comes up and downright hot later in the morning. In any climate, we may have to put up with spring showers that can dampen the vegetation and ultimately the hunter.

Ideally several types of camouflage clothing are needed. We may hunt Merriam's where we sit against the brown base of a ponderosa pine or an outcropping of rimrock or we might hunt the Osceola and sit against a green palmetto. Therefore, we need several colors or patterns of camouflage clothing. The handiest type of clothing then is a reversible—brown camouflage and green camouflage—cotton jumpsuit or pants and jacket large enough to go over any combination of clothing that supplies warmth and or waterproofing.

The only problem with this kind of clothing available today is that it usually uses a long zipper for a closure which is fine when zipped up but when partly open the zippers are shiny enough to alert the gobbler. I had

In many parts of the country, "layering" is the way to dress for early spring hunting. You can take off extra clothing, but you can't add what you don't have with you.

the zipper removed from the jacket of my reversible suit and a set of heavy duty black snaps installed.

If it's cold, I wear layers of cardigan-style clothes underneath my jacket so I can open up or button up, depending on my activity. I wear either a pair of soft, comfortable pants or a set of polypropylene (wicking) long underwear under my camouflage pants. If it's raining, I wear a set of Gore-Tex rain clothes under my cotton camouflage suit.

Most waterproof camouflage clothing is noisy in the woods or brush, but does well when worn under cotton. For this same reason (brush noise), I seldom use down or fiber-filled vests or jackets unless worn underneath. The best bets are cardigan-type wool sweaters and pile-lined woolen vests which are available in camouflage and may be worn under your camouflage coveralls or suit. In the south, or during late spring in the North, it is often not necessary to wear anything but a T-shirt underneath, but it is wise to use one available in camouflage so you can open up the front of your jacket. This reduces the possibility of spooking the turkey with that splash of white T-shirt. It also reduces the danger of being shot.

There are many other choices in camouflage suits with many patterns and colors to choose from, including the military patterns available in surplus cloth and clothing. There is a new "Trebark" pattern which is excellent for most set-ups.

To me, the best all-around pattern and color is the large mixed pattern found in chamois cloth clothing. This clothing is also very comfortable and quiet, but the fabrics to date do not wear well, though the splotches of light tans, greens, and browns blend with most backgrounds at any time of the year.

A turkey hunter's suit can't have too many pockets. Pockets keep calls separate, hold extra shells, sandwiches, and other goodies that we will talk about in this chapter.

Other items to wear turkey hunting are boots or shoes, socks, gloves, a hat, and a mask if you don't use face paint.

It's not necessary to wear camouflage boots; usually they are buried in ground cover and not visible at any distance. However, don't wear white or bright-colored boots, shoes, or laces. My favorite all-around hunting boot is the rubber-bottom leather-top pac.

Socks will show when you are sitting and your pant legs are drawn up. Brown, tan, gray, and green socks are as easy to find in whatever material you prefer as the brightly colored kind. Avoid wearing white athletic socks.

Gloves are a must. The parts of the human body that stand out in the turkey woods, or a duck blind, are your hands and face. Gloves are available in camouflage, but this is not totally necessary. Any dull leather glove or cotton work glove in brown will work fine.

A hat should be in your favorite camouflage style. Be careful not to use a color that contrasts greatly with the rest of your outfit. If you are bow-hunting make sure the brim does not get in the way of your anchor point.

Finally, a mask is as important as any part of your outfit. If you use camouflage face paint instead, experiment and find the kind that comes off easily and does not bother your skin. Many types of camouflage face masks are on the market. The choice comes down to the mask that hides your face, but gives the best visibility, including good peripheral vision, is comfortable, allows you to get a call in your mouth or to your mouth, and does not cause your glasses to steam up (if you wear them). My favorite is the type that goes across the bridge of my nose and is held in place with a piece of elastic, enabling me to look out between the top of it and the brim of my hat. I cut mine just short enough to cover my chin and throat so that I can get to my mouth easily with my tube call or yelpers.

This hunter risks scaring off a trophy—or even getting shot at. The white T-shirt defeats the purpose of the camo cover.

Good camouflage clothes should be practical, comfortable, and provide you with the confidence that you are well hidden in your surroundings. As with your clothes, anything else you wear or have with you that shows should either be in camouflage or of a muted (browns, greens, etc.) color.

There are certain accessories that are almost as important as all others previously mentioned. In the chapter on turkey calls we mentioned that the big box call can be fragile, hard to get at, and noisy. If carried in your

Note the difference this makes. Camo clothing is available in many styles, to fit your preferences and the cover you're hunting. It may be a good idea to buy a brown-green reversible outfit.

pocket or pack this is true. In 1976 I designed and produced the original box call holster which is now made by several manufacturers and comes in both leather with sheepskin cushions and also in heavy camouflage fabric with pile cushions. This holster is just as important as the box call and keeps the call handy, safe, and quiet when carrying. These holsters also

Bright socks can spook birds. Be sure to wear muted colors that won't show up if your pants hike up when you sit down.

have leg tie downs so the box call can be removed from the snug holster and replaced with one hand.

You can spend a lot of time on your fanny when turkey hunting and as you get a little older you will find that keeping dry and comfortable is

Hat and face masking are recommended—but this hunter could do without the patch on his headgear.

essential when trying to sit still. There are several foam-filled, waterproof cushions available. The best are part of a vest or a pack that folds out of the way when not in use. A small, camouflage day pack is also handy and when the pack and the seat cushion are combined, ideal. The one I use is made by Albert McMillan of Carthage, Mississippi and combines a game

Everything in its place makes you more efficient—and potentially productive—in the woods. This hunter has his box calls inserted in holsters with his Mc Millan vest.

bag (which serves as a pack) with a vest with pockets and shell loops and a fold-down, waterproof cushion. I have never gone turkey hunting without it, and I keep all my gear in it so I don't have to fumble around searching for things in the dark.

If you need to carry water or juice along—important in those states

An ordinary folding knife and a pair of pruning shears will make easy work of the initial dressing of your bird.

where you can hunt spring gobblers all day—the best container is an unbreakable plastic bottle. It should be kept in your pack rather than as a canteen on your belt. You will have enough on your belt, and a canteen is in the way when you sit.

Another thing to include in your gear is a turkey "tote" of some kind. Many are on the market and all help in keeping spurs or bloody heads out of your hands and the weight on your shoulders. A small knife is important in an emergency and also to field dress your turkey. A folding knife in a sheath or in your pocket is less in the way when you are seated. The gut hooks which come on some are useful in removing the intestines, but you will have to use your hand to remove the gizzard, heart, and liver. Don't consider the hook a necessity.

A good, light set of pruners is always handy. They are used for quietly snipping small plants and branches that poke your bottom and sides when you sit. They are used to snip off small branches, etc., that might rub against your clothing as you sneak along, trying to get closer to your bird. They can be used to make a small blind of branches stuck in the ground around you and finally when you are preparing the bird for the freezer they are handy for clipping off wings, feet, etc.

A pocket camera as described previously is nice to have with you. Toilet paper can sometimes be even more appropriate to have along. Bug repellent is a must in many areas during the spring hunt. A small plastic bag containing sandpaper and chalk should be included if you are carrying a box call. Another should contain sandpaper or abrasive pad if you are carrying a slate call and still another should provide extra diaphragms if you are carrying a tube call.

If you have a shiny watch, cover it with a camouflage band or cover. If you want to have your gobbler mounted by a taxidermist carry a plastic garbage bag—more on this later.

Look at the tag provided with your license for attaching to the turkey. Some are self-sticking but others must be tied, and for these I carry a couple of garbage bag wire twists. Many other things should be considered, depending on where you are hunting and the duration of the hunt: compass, local topo maps, flashlight, matches, first-aid kit, snake bite kit, and so on.

In your car or camp, or on your person if you are hunting in a state that requires the filling out of your turkey tag before the bird is moved, you will want a pen for filling out tags. A tape measure, and if you are so inclined, a set of applications for the record book, plus a good scale should also be in your car or camp. I recommend a Chatillon spring scale used by most fish and game departments.

Last but not least, and I am sure by now somebody has wondered about my not mentioning them so far, are locator type calls—owl calls, crow calls, etc., that are used to get an answer at various times of the day or night. We will discuss these at length in the next chapter.

Chapter 8

HUNTING BASICS

The basic steps for hunting spring turkeys are: 1) pre-season preparation; 2) finding the gobbler or locating turkeys; 3) scouting and roosting; 4) "set-up" (establishing a position) and calling, and 5) harvesting the gobbler. Actual strategy under different conditions is dealt with in the following chapter.

Pre-season preparation starts with the gathering of equipment discussed in previous chapters. This is the time to make modifications where necessary. It is the time to get to know your gun, bow or camera. It is time to sight in and pattern your shotgun or practice with your bow.

If you are a beginner, it is the time to learn as much about turkey hunting as possible by reading books and magazine articles and listening to instructional tapes available to the new turkey hunter. It's also the time when experienced and inexperienced hunters practice their calling.

Once you know how to make basic calls on the calling devices you select, listen to one of the cassettes available that are actual recordings of wild turkeys making their various calls. It is far better to imitate the real thing than to imitate an expert who is trying to sound like a turkey. To imitate another person is getting the story second hand. If you are not sure of how you sound, record yourself on a cassette (outdoors gives less distortion) and compare your sounds with the real thing.

When you hear an actual recording you will be amazed at how differently one bird sounds from another and how seemingly imperfect they sometimes sound. This will also help you realize that turkeys can make some awful sounding noises.

Don't stop calling if you make a bad call or mistake. If you follow it by a decent one the turkey will never know the difference. But listen for the

Here's a typical setting where you might find a strutting Eastern tom.

rhythm, the timing, and get together with your friends and give each other constructive criticism on your calling. Don't go out to the area you expect to hunt and try to see if it works. You only educate the gobblers.

Step two, just before the season, you want to find a gobbler or gobblers. Turkeys do not necessarily stay in the same spot where they were last fall and winter and, more importantly, they will often be in places where they were absent in fall or winter. Remember in the chapter about his life cycle, the gobbler is seeking his own hens and a "territory" to contain them; the flocks are breaking up. Locating gobblers is a matter of time and common sense. Not all gobblers have distinctive "territories," some are very mobile. You will, however, often find gobblers where you found other gobblers in previous springs. Spring gobblers are found where the hens are and the hens are in, or near, good nesting areas.

Gobblers are more obvious in their early morning strutting and gob-bling before the season than they will be under hunting pressure. They are often heard and seen in the corner of a meadow or field doing their thing. People traveling the roads during those hours see them and those who are up and about hear them. Truckers, ranchers, farmers, and school bus drivers as well as people who talk with them, such as owners of diners, gas stations, etc., are good sources of information. In many cases local fish

Finding a roosting bird will give you a very helpful headstart for hunting the next morning. Putting a bird to bed is also an added adventure on a turkey hunt. This is typical Florida roosting cover.

and game department personnel are also sources, as are sporting goods store operators and license agents.

Once you determine where the old gobbler was seen or heard, the next step is to locate the property owner. Only if you are certain the property is public land should you neglect this step.

Management areas such as those found in the south and west are available, sometimes with a fee, and information on the game they contain can be obtained from the local manager or biologist in charge. Such areas are sometimes crowded with hunters.

If you are willing to make the effort of finding private property owners and seek hunting permission, you can enjoy uncrowded, high quality hunting as well as acquire a new friend who will often show or tell you where the game is.

I believe landowner permission to be of the utmost importance, even if the land is unposted. If you are hunting away from home, local laws and customs can be very different from those with which you are familiar. If you make a mistake and end up in court, it is their court, not yours. There are places where even adjoining farmers or ranchers never set foot on their neighbor's property without permission; and permission must be current and not something granted a year ago. There is no fun in being run off by an irate owner. There is great satisfaction, however, in having a successful hunt because of a good relationship with the person whose crops and habitat made it possible.

Here are roosting sites for Rio Grande turkeys.

We know the turkey is there, and we don't have to look over our shoulder while looking for him. Now we can enjoy a bonus hunt, the pre-season scouting expedition. This means going into the woods without your turkey call, rather taking your crow call or owl hooter. There is a tremendous temptation to practice the hunt with your turkey calls. I have had hunters walk into my shop to ask what they were doing wrong because three times they called in this gobbler then on opening day and the following days he did not respond.

"I know he didn't see me," they say.

If you saw him, chances are he saw you. And even if he did not, he knows he should have seen a hen. It doesn't take him long to know something is wrong. "Locator" calls allow you to get gobbles out of him without calling him in. His territorial nature and habit of announcing this to the world whenever a loud sound is heard, particularly if it is made by another territorial bird such as an owl or crow, makes it possible. Some believe this is due to harassment by each of these birds at a more vulnerable stage in the gobbler's life. I believe that when a gobbler is in a gobbling mood he will answer any natural, distinctive nearby noise. They will even answer woodpeckers.

In scouting, spend enough time not only to find the area where he roosts, but to learn if he already has hens with him. And if he does, where do they lead him. This practice not only increases your time and fun in the woods, but also gives you an inside edge on bagging him on opening day.

The chances are that because hunting pressure does not yet exist he will be sounding off frequently. When the tom is not gobbling on his own, you can get him to answer your imitation of a loud raucous crow call during the day, or before dawn and at dusk, the barred owl or great horned owl. (The great horned owl is most common in the west.)

Pattern his movements. Determine where he goes and when. Find his strutting ground. In the northeast it is usually a knoll where the woods are open, and ground level visibility is excellent. Short grasses and spring beauty often comprise the forest floor, and nut and seed producing trees such as oaks, hop hornbean, and ash are present. It's here the hens can stroll about picking up insects, seeds and tubers at will. The gobbler can strut his stuff, occasionally mating with one of the hens.

When you know his movement patterns, you won't be done in on opening morning when you find another hunter set-up near his roost. You can simply give the other guy his room and move off to the strutting ground or a good spot along the way and have as good a chance, or better, to get the bird.

The going can get a little tough when hunting Merriam's turkeys, but a stand of pines like this on a mountain slope would be a good place to look.

But what if you work during the day and have little time to scout or have just arrived in a new hunting area? Roosting a turkey can be profitable in all types of turkey habitat. All turkeys, except incubating and brooding hens, roost in trees. When experienced turkey hunters arrive in new territory, the first thing they want to know is whether they got there in time to roost a gobbler.

Roosting areas are more obvious in some parts of the country than others. The Florida turkey likes to roost over water, as mentioned earlier, and is usually found at night in the cypress trees that make up a "head" which is fairly easy to pick out of the surrounding landscape. It also roosts next to "back ups" (areas of flooded timber) around lake shores.

The Rio Grande, usually limited in its roosting cover, often spends an entire season in one roost. Merriam's often use the same roost over and over but because they have plenty of areas to roost, they may vary roosting sights.

Most Merriam's roosts are in pines on the slopes of side canyons not far from a water source in the main canyon.

The roosts of Eastern turkeys are the hardest to locate. They are often found within gliding distance of the opening where the gobbler struts early in the morning. Sometimes, roost areas can be located by finding drop-

Ben Conger uses an owl hooter to locate birds. This is a favorite and effective call for trying to single out a bird.

pings and feathers under the roosting trees. When you are in the area of roosting turkeys at dusk, they can be heard "flying up." This is a commonly used method to find a roost in Florida. However, when in an area where the roost is uncertain you have to listen for roost talk, particularly gobbling.

The most common method of finding a roost is to make the old Tom gobble. On the roost, the gobbler will often gobble at another gobble, an owl hooting, coyotes and loud high pitched cuts or yelps. It's safe to use these last hen calls at this time because he is going to stay in the tree until dawn. Also, these calls carry farther than the other sounds. In Western canyons we have roosted Merriam's that were a mile and a half away.

In the East the most popular call for enticing an answer is that of the barred owl made with a "hooter" or with your own voice if you are adept at this.

Out West the "hooter" gets more reaction from coyotes. My method out West is to start with a gobble, and then, if no answer, the longer range cuts and cackles on a mouth yelper or tube call. It is important to remember that three to five minutes or more should elapse between attempts to call.

Wherever gobblers are roosted on a quiet night it is possible to cover a lot of country by driving around after dark, stopping at a likely spot, and after letting everything quiet down give it a try. Some turkeys will gobble back all night if you want to stay with it. You can, of course, roost a bird before dawn the same way you can after dark. Sometimes they will answer then when they wouldn't the evening before. This has happened many times in the northeast. I have gone back in the morning after having had a luckless night, only because I was convinced a gobbler was there somewhere, and got an immediate response.

Now that you know where he roosts, you are ready for the next step—setting-up and calling.

Once that turkey is gobbling, you should get as close as you can without spooking him. If because of your scouting or previous experience you have a good idea where he will fly down (often an opening or a clearing) you should set-up there. If you don't have any idea, then you should get to a place at the same elevation or slightly above him. Or if you know something about his habits you want to be in a place the gobbler wants to go or has gone before in the company of his hens.

How many times has your calling been terrific, but the old bird seems to have other places to go? You want to be in one of those other places.

Find a comfortable set-up that has a big tree, thick bush, stump, ledge or something you can sit in front of, breaking up your outline and blending with your background. In picking your spot make sure there is no thick brush or natural barrier the gobbler has to come through to get to you. He likes good ground-level visibility, both so as to see, but also to let the hens see him. If it is a damp morning, he will skirt wet vegetation.

Here's a hunter in a typical setup. He's resting comfortably against a large stump, with his call in hand and his gun on his lap. Some hunters prefer a full head net that covers the eyes, and there are models to accommodate hunters who wear glasses.

It is also a good idea, if possible, to be in an area where there are enough good-sized trees to allow him to pass behind once within range (almost imperative with a bow), enabling you to get your gun on him without being seen. In many cases this is impossible, and you have to wait for the gobbler to turn away in strut, tail hiding his head, to get your gun up. With

This could be a dangerous situation for the hunter because his back and head are exposed.

the right set-up in a place he wants to go or pass through, your calling does not have to be good in order to lure him in range.

Normally, the sun will not yet be a factor, but when it is low and bright a gobbler is hesitant to come straight in to it. Rather, he will circle to get the sun out of his eyes and this should be taken into consideration. You can keep the sun out of your eyes by sitting in a shadow.

This doesn't mean you can goof up entirely, but good woodsmanship leading to a good set-up is far more important than great calling. It's also good to remember when you set-up to try to get your best field of fire. In other words, if you're right handed, sit with your left shoulder in the direction you expect him to come from. This gives you a full 180-degrees of motion. Gobblers have a habit of circling you.

The same set-up criteria should be followed any time you are about to call a gobbler. It is very important to have picked out and moved to a proper set-up before trying any calls to start a gobbler even if you are just trying to find one. This of course does not pertain to using a locator (crow or owl) call. Unsuccessful and discouraged, I have been caught out in the open too many times when I sounded some yelps to see if a gobbler was around—he was, and he was always too close—to ever ignore this rule again. Sometimes you will have a turkey gobble at you at close range

Calling is fun, and many hunters do it periodically—and casually—as they stroll through the woods. It's smarter, however, to pick your spot so you can hunker down quickly if you get a response.

because he heard your steps and thought you were another turkey. And usually, by the time you both recover, he is gone.

After setting-up on a roosted turkey, and allowing a reasonable time for things to settle down, you should make your first call. Don't rush it, but make it before he leaves the roost. Some feel that in heavily hunted areas it is better not to call until after he flies down. He feels much safer when he flies down to an observed hen.

This first call can be two or three very soft tree yelps that can be made with a mouth or tube call or slate. To a human these calls are not audible more than 20-30 yards, but a gobbler on the roost hears well, far better than when on the ground, and he is listening for this sound. Also, his hearing is attuned to it.

If the caller is not familiar with the tree call, or prefers, like myself, to use a soft cluck or cluck and purr instead, this can be equally effective. Do not make loud yelps or cackles at this time. After you make the first call of your choice, the gobbler may either respond immediately, sometimes with a double or triple gobble in which case your job may be almost done, or he may suddenly cease his gobbling, leaving the caller to wonder if he has done something wrong.

Rather, the old bird has probably heard just what he wanted and has nothing more to say. This is particularly true later in the season when gobbling is kept to a minimum. It is important in either case, unless you are quite far away from him (more than 200 yards), to cease your calling under these conditions. You may be tempted to call again, but usually all

Here's a well-camouflaged hunter. The bow is almost invisible. Some archers prefer to have their spare arrows on the bow, however. It might be difficult for this hunter to reach quickly for a second shaft if he misses and the bird offers a second chance.

this does is keep him on the roost even strutting and displaying there, waiting for that eager young hen to show.

Most times you will hear him fly down. If he does not gobble when he lands, get ready, he is likely to be heading right for you and the next thing you may hear is his spits and drumming, or in the West the sound of his wing tips thrust into the ground as he struts.

If he gobbles when he gets to the ground you might venture a short series of yelps or several clucks or even a cackle to head him your way rather than toward another hen he may have heard. If he continues to gobble and not approach your position, it is time to use the mating cackle.

A word of caution here. I believe that with mature gobblers this is the only time you should use the cackle unless you are very experienced with it. A hen also cackles sometimes when flying down from her roost or to her roost at dusk. Lovett Williams, author of *The Book of the Wild Turkey,* says cackling is usually associated with flying. The "fly-down cackle," as it is often referred to, is different from the mating cackle and in late morning this cackle often gets gobblers to respond but is unnatural and out of place then. This is a mute point, however, because often just

This is a good idea that you don't see often. In some situations you may have only a quick kneeling shot, and knee pads make it a lot easier.

picking up the tempo of a series of yelps excites the gobbler. The actual description or definition of a mating cackle compared to the fly-down cackle is best described on the Master Tape sold by Penns Woods.

I have had experiences that lead me to believe care should be taken in using the cackle later in the morning. Once I was trying to lure in a magnificent Merriam's, that was in the company of six hens. Having had no success, I tried a cackle. The gobbler immediately responded with a booming gobble and snapped into his strut, but the six hens that had been

This photo shows how handy knee pads can be. It's tough to shoot a bow from a sitting position.

placidly feeding took off on the run leading my perplexed half-strutting gobbler away in chase. I believe my cackle was wrong and they knew hens don't fly down cackling at mid-morning.

The cackle, done right, has worked on many gobblers and turned the trick when competition is nearby, but so has a fast series of cutts followed by a couple of yelps or just a faster, choppier series of yelps than that of the competition.

Once the gobbler is on the ground for a while, and on through the day, the calls that are used are a short series of yelps with or without clucks. And sometimes, to egg him on, little whines and purrs. Remember, when a turkey is in close proximity with another, they don't use loud yelps to communicate but rather soft clucks, whines, and purrs.

Early in the season, as we mentioned before, the hens are more vocal and can be heard doing quite a bit of loud yelping. As the season wears on this yelping is replaced by soft whines, yelps and clucks. At this time, loud yelps and cackles sound wrong to the gobbler and even if not spooked he probably won't come in.

You've set-up right. Your calling was right. There he is! You can hardly believe it. Your heart is pounding so hard you are sure he can hear it. He is about to step behind a tree and you will be able to get your gun on him and when he reappears it will be all over.

But it's not over yet. And far too many gobblers are lost at this point so on to the last step.

Are the hens around? Don't forget them. They have eyes too, a couple of alarm putts and he will vanish from behind the tree. Know where they are when you move to shoot.

Is he in easy range or has your excitement, anticipation and his size made you too eager? Is there a clear shot or have you not even noticed the brush, branches, or small trees that can blow your pattern to bits? Change your point of focus and make sure. And when you are ready to pull that trigger this is not the time to still be admiring him or measuring his beard over the bead of your gun. Get your cheek on the buttstock, sight down that rib like it was a match target rifle, pick a point at the base of his warty head and only then pull the trigger.

You can still lose him. Get to him as fast as you can, turkeys have recovery powers beyond imagination. Don't try to pick him up, unless you want a powerful wing across your face, put your foot on his head and neck and make sure he is dead. Then you can stop shaking and start congratulating yourself for a job well done.

Chapter 9

STRATEGY FOR THE FOUR STAGES OF A GOBBLER'S SPRING BEHAVIOR

As humans we have a highly developed brain and reasoning power. Skilled psychiatrists can predict fairly closely our behavior under given circumstances. Turkeys have small, undeveloped brains. The only thing predictable about their behavior is that they are unpredictable. For this reason any statements about turkey behavior made in this book can be wrong as well as right. A successful turkey hunter must be a lucky turkey hunter. However, some understanding of what takes place can help stack the deck in your favor.

Across the nation spring gobbler hunting spans three months. Thus, you may find yourself hunting a gobbler during one of several stages of spring behavior. We know, for instance, that the change in hours of light as opposed to darkness is what triggers the biological mechanism controlling breeding. But this is altered to some extent by climatic conditions. A cold, wet spring can delay mating; a warm dry spring, may hasten it.

Local conditions can also be a factor. One year in April I hunted Merriam's in a five-mile long, north-south running Wyoming canyon. There was snow in the north end but just a few patches in the south end. The turkeys in the north end were still in mixed flocks; those in the south end had split up, a gobbler on the head of each side canyon strutting with his hens.

The gobblers would not be hunted in the canyon's north end the same way as those in its south end. Different tactics are used in hunting gobblers in mixed flocks; hunting gobblers gathering hens; hunting gobblers with harems; and hunting gobblers after the hens have left and are sitting on their nests.

Seldom in the East, but often in the West, you will be hunting gobblers during the first stage or in mixed flocks. Merriam's and Rio Grande flocks can be made up of 50 to 100 birds. I hunted Merriam's when there were at least 12 mature gobblers in a flock. With a flock like this, you may see this many strutting birds on one hillside. When turkeys are in flocks it takes more scouting and roosting to find them than when they are spread out over an area.

Western flocks also tend to cover a lot of ground in a day. I once followed a flock of Merriam's up and down one steep-sided canyon after another until I quit only to find them back in the same roost that night. For this reason it is always feast or famine when hunting turkey flocks. Once you locate the flock you will find the gobblers do not respond the way you would hope. They are gobbling and strutting but are reluctant to come to you when they are surrounded by hens.

The gobblers are not yet driving off jakes and pay little attention to other mature gobblers except for the long-since established pecking order. Also, they are not interested in gathering more hens as they are already overwhelmed by them. Before the flock splits up there may be as many as 100 hens in it. Thus, normal calling does little more than evoke gobbles and only then when it is done a little louder than the real hens are doing or is done during a quiet spell.

The flock is usually very vocal at this time, particularly during the first few hours of the day, and this gives you a chance to get close or even get in a position ahead of it.

Once the flock is in your vicinity, the trick is not to try enticing the gobbler but to call in a group of hens. The hens are very gregarious at this time; for the most part, they have lived together as a flock since birth. Also, they have established a pecking order. When you hear a group of them yelping, try to imitate them and yelp back, but do it more often and louder than they. If when they answer back a "run of yelps" gets raspier and more urgent try to do the same. When hens are heard clucking, you cluck. And, when because of your refusal to join them, their clucks get sharper and more annoyed you do the same. In either case the chances are

Setting up properly is part of the strategy for bettering the chance of bringing home a trophy wild turkey. Camo gear is essential.

they will head your way either to settle things or out of obedience. Where they go one or more gobblers will follow, strutting. All the turkey talk will definitely hold his attention.

I have had good luck with both yelps and clucks in both circumstances. Earlier in the book we mentioned the two mature gobblers fighting it out over their dead comrade. It happened like this: I found a flock of Merriam's and got above them. Hidden at the base of a pine, I watched several groups of gobblers and hens cross below me. When I yelped, they gobbled, but gave no other sign of interest. When the next group showed up, I started imitating them—yelping on a Perfection Raspy D mouth call. When I got an answer I just kept up a steady series of urgent raspy yelps, filling in with some clucks on my 1-Hander Slate. It didn't take long for six hens, gobbler in tow, to head up the hill toward me. I continued non-stop yelping even after they went out of sight in a shallow ravine and only quit when they came up over the edge opposite me. I sat still as the hens walked and pecked their way by me, splitting up either side of where I sat. After they passed I had only to raise my gun and shoot as the gobbler's head appeared over the edge.

With the shot he dropped out of sight, but the range was only 10 to 15 yards and I heard him flop. I ran over and stood on the edge of the ravine looking down at him flopping in the bottom. And there beside him were two more mature gobblers, who, after giving him a peck or two, started going at each other in earnest to see who would inherit his share of the hens.

A later hunt found me in the same situation. I heard the flock and crept to the top of a rimrock outcropping overlooking the area where the birds were gobbling. I sneaked through an opening and sat down between a pine on my left and the outcropping on my right. There were turkeys all around. A large gobbler strutted on a hillside about 70-80 yards away. He was being copied by four or five other mature birds I could see spread out in the area. None were within range.

I then heard hens clucking down in the bottom to my left, I started to do the same on my 1-Hander slate call. We clucked back and forth for awhile and finally one old boss hen decided to let me have it with a series of sharp, annoyed clucks. I did the same and soon heard them heading for me. I heard them walking just the other side of the pine on my left when a nice gobbler came strutting around the corner not 20 feet below me. With the shot he flopped to the bottom as the others gobbled at every flop. I let the now alerted flock work its way out of sight and went down and retrieved my turkey.

I certainly can't say this method always works, nor is it the only way, but calling up the hens of a mixed flock works for me.

We will talk about calling hens again, but you don't have to think of it when the next stage of spring gobbler behavior occurs, the gathering of hens.

Note the position of the hunter in relation to his fallen bird. Ideally, shots are at 40 yards or less.

Because of the gobbling activity, this is one of the two times you can really enjoy hunting. Also, you often get to hunt all gobblers North, South, East, and West at this stage. Sometimes it only takes one or two days for the gobblers to go from stage one to stage two. Biologists talk about the two peaks of gobbling activity and this is the first of these.

The gobbler is trying to attract, round up and contain his own group of hens. He may take hens from the flock and choose the territory he will dominate or he may leave the flock, pick a territory and try attracting hens there. This new territory will now contain him and his hens in an area limited generally to the area where nesting will take place.

Therefore, the wide-ranging Western birds will no longer travel much farther than what is needed for food and water and nesting habitat. And the dominant gobbler in the given area, either Eastern or Western, will stay in the area no matter how much pressure is put on him until he has been killed or the hens have left him and are incubating.

During this stage the gobbler is trying his best to attract hens. This is the peak of gobbling activity and gobbling may continue all day. To a gobbler, any hen sounds are worth investigating in hopes it will add to the harem. Sometimes you find a gobbler looking for his first hen and his actions at this time would label him as "hot." A "hot" gobbler can be called in with little experience. Often these birds seem to abandon all caution and so called "wildness." However, older birds at this time of temporary foolishness can still prove difficult to call. These birds, often Eastern or Florida gobblers that have lived through heavy hunter pressure, can still challenge the best.

Generally speaking, the more experienced the bird the subtler the calling must be and the more careful the selection of a calling spot must be. This is why most of the long, sharp, hook-spurred gobblers are only taken by the best of hunters no matter what stage the spring hunt is in.

Because of their constant gobbling, the males are obviously easier to find at this stage and in some cases they will go to great efforts to find you.

One day I was working along the top of the rimrock of a Black Hills canyon. I stopped every 100 yards or so yelping loudly on my tube. In the canyon bottom a friend of mine, David Baldinger, was waiting beside his pickup and heard me calling. Also, unknown to me, he heard a gobbler responding far up the canyon. As I worked my way up, the gobbler was coming down answering my calls. According to David, he watched this gobbler fly across three side canyons in his effort to get to me. I finally heard him and was able to work him in across a small clearing atop the rimrock. Sometimes, however I fail to call a Vermont bird across a shallow ditch.

Gobblers may also have one or two hens with them at this stage and still be seeking more, or at least have an interest in hen sounds he hears. If he doesn't come in readily, you may have to change your position. This is best done after you stop calling for a while to see what he will do. Often, stopping your calling and being perfectly quiet will make him come in to

Get to your fallen trophy quickly. Supposedly dead birds have been known to thunder off before the hunter could compose himself for another shot.

see where you have gone. He was interested but, having one or two hens with him, was not going to go out of his way as long as he knew you were still around. If you move on him without waiting you may hear him sound off again at your old position.

One spring I heard a Vermont bird open up late in the morning. He was at the head of an overgrown pasture in the middle of which a ravine lead to a brook. Large timber grew on the edges and banks of the ravine. Brush and a few old apple trees stood in the pasture but there was little cover to conceal a moving hunter.

I called and got answers from the gobbler and a hen he was with. He walked back and forth in the heavy timber. Since I seemed unable to lure him out, I decided to circle and come up the brook into the ravine. I got there and heard the hen yelping and cutting like crazy so I set-up on the other side of the ravine. I was just about to call when I heard a gobble back across the pasture where I had just been. I figured there were now two hens on my side so I mimicked the hen's yelps and cutts. The gobbler answered, but still stayed over there looking for the new hen. Every time I called, the real hen wandered over to the edge of the ravine. Not wanting her in my lap, I would quit calling. Finally, she decided to come over anyway and I had to wait until she went out of sight in the ravine bottom. I then opened up for all I was worth, but the gobbler was taking his own sweet time coming back. The hen reappeared and walked right up to my feet. I didn't dare move; I had my gun pointing across the ravine. Finally, she made me out and without moving off, started to putt. I saw the old gobbler's head poke through the "hard hack" as he tried to see what was going on but I never got a shot. I would have had him all to myself if I had stayed long enough where I started.

For the most part, however, gobblers gathering hens provide at least half the classic hunts described in the stories you hear and articles you read.

Gobblers, however, at stage three, with their hens as they have become a unit, can be very difficult to hunt. Because of the apparent lack of gobbling and interest by gobblers, many hunters quit hunting, feeling the gobbling season has ended. Of course, this is not a prime hunting time, but success can be had, particularly if you know a little about what is happening and have a few tricks to try.

The gobbler has now settled in with his harem of two to six or more hens and has little interest in more. He is with them all day, has bred each at least once and except for one or more of them sneaking off for a short while to lay an egg she is back, and he has never learned to count. She will be with him until roosting time and then she will be there all night with the other hens just a few trees away. At dawn he can tell by their soft yelps and clucks that they are there and he may gobble once on the roost before flying down to let them know where he is or he may not even bother to gobble.

They now know each other well and fly down and move off together usually over the same path day after day. Little talk is necessary to keep in touch. The hens can be heard scratching and walking and occasionally making soft whiney yelps and soft clucks and purrs. The gobbler struts his stuff and seldom gobbles. If he does gobble, and if he is an old bird, he may gobble so softly it cannot be heard much more than 100 yards. It's all that is needed to keep in touch with his hens.

Once I had one of these gobblers strutting on the opposite bank no more than 45 yards away. When he gobbled I wasn't sure if it was him or another bird that was out of sight. If I hadn't seen him gobble I would not have known. The first time this happened to me I thought the old bird had some shot in his tonsils but I have seen it enough now to realize they often do this.

When turkeys are in this stage the most important thing you can do is have an idea of their daily pattern which we discussed earlier. If you know this pattern you have several ways of trying for the big bird.

The first is to call him off the roost before his hens can get to him. This requires knowledge of where he roosts and where he usually flies down to.

One spring, a large Vermont gobbler gave fits to the farmer who owned the roadside cornfield where he strutted with his four hens each morning. Hunter after hunter asked for permission to hunt this bird. Several of us hunted him unsuccessfully for the first few days of the season. The gobbler was just not interested. He gobbled tantalizing on his roost, but when he gobbled after flying down he did it so softly we couldn't figure out where he was. The third day I tried him I found his roost. In the dark, I moved in close and set-up against a maple top at the base of a ledgey hillside overlooking the cornfield.

The old bird and his hens were roosting in some trees in the ledges from where they could glide down into the field. Just a few yards of woods and a stone wall separated me from this field. Shortly after setting-up I made a cluck or two and the old bird gobbled. I made no further sound but he continued to gobble. Then I heard someone coming. The gobbler stopped and a hunter walked by. After all settled down again I clucked and to my joy he opened up again. A little while later I heard the beating of wings and the gobbler glided over my head toward the field. Before his feet hit the ground I made a quick series of three yelps on a Quaker Boy "Old Turk" mouth call.

It worked because he immediately ran in my direction. Over the wall he came and into the pattern of my 3-inch magnum. At the shot, four hens flew from their roost above me. But on the ground lay a beautiful Vermont gobbler weighing 22 pounds and sporting an exceptionally thick 9½-inch beard and spurs 1¼-inches long. Mounted, he adorns my office.

The second method is to "wait him out." At some time during the morning the hens will leave to lay an egg. Eventually, some will leave to incubate her eggs and not return. Depending on the number of hens with the gobbler, there are periods when he is left alone for a while. When alone, he is receptive, but it is difficult for you to be in the right place at the right time. What you can do, however, is let him know in advance you are around. He'll remember you when he is alone. This is best done near his roost as the following story reveals.

I tried calling in a New York gobbler several days in vain, but I found where he roosted and I knew where he went during the morning. However it was almost impossible to get near the roost in the dry leaves without the chance of spooking him. He roosted just over the eastern side of a low open hardwood ridge and upon flying down assembled with his hens on top of the ridge then traveled west down the other side across a brook and then out a long parallel ridge.

I moved as close as I dared and then set-up but did no calling. He gobbled several times on the roost then flew down, gathered up his two hens and headed west. As soon as I could I moved to the assembly area and made one loud, short cackle. There was no answer; I made myself comfortable for the long wait.

About 8:30 I heard a gobble way out on the other ridge. He had probably just lost one, or maybe both, hens. At 9:10 he gobbled again. This time he was on his way back. I answered with a snappy series of yelps. Soon I saw him strutting down the other side of the brook, heading for me. A few more clucks on my slate had him gobbling and strutting in earnest only about 50 yards away. Just then out of the corner of my eye I saw two turkeys running in my direction. "His hens coming back," I thought. But no, it was a pair of jakes trying to get to me ahead of the old boy. They were successful and after running me down started putting in alarm. I was left with the choice of a jake or nothing at all so I shot a jake. (The old gobbler would have been mine though, and all because he remembered that hen in the bush he left behind when the birds in hand had left him.)

The third method that we touched on before is "calling in the hens." As previously related in the account in the chapter on Turkey calls, hens will come to sharp clucking. I don't believe they react to any form of yelping at this point in the season as well as they do to sharp clucking or cutting. Yelps can be used to fill in occasionally, though. Again you must be in their immediate area.

Whether they come to throw out the intruder (hens are territorial), or to join a friend, I don't know. If you hear one hen making more noise than the others, a hen making louder yelps, sometimes coarser at the end, or sharper clucks, there is a good chance that she is a "boss" or dominant hen. I have found that if I imitate her I usually get an immediate reaction on her part as she aggressively approaches.

I've called up hens with gobblers, but I've also called up hens that for some reason were alone. I know that in one instance the gobbler was killed the previous day. I have kept lone hens around for quite a while, hoping all the chatter would attract a gobbler. I use a lot of clucks or a continuous cluck-and-purr sequence. If I start to lose the hen, a couple of nasal sounding yelps used in combination with the other calls often renews their interest.

The last method is to "challenge" the gobbler. There are only two occasions when you should gobble: the first, already discussed, is when you gobble to locate or roost a turkey; the other is to challenge a dominant turkey on his home grounds.

Any other time you make a gobble while turkey hunting you are inviting potential danger from turkey stalkers. Also, the gobble tells jakes or non-dominant gobblers in the area that they are not welcome.

A challenge must be made in the boss gobbler's territory and preferably close in. If you work a turkey enough to know he has hens with him and is not interested in gathering more, you should also know where he goes with those hens. Set-up in his area and if you hear the birds or think they are there, try your gobble. If you get an answer, follow it with another gobble immediately. This constitutes the challenge. Each time the turkey gobbles, answer with your gobble and get ready. He should show up, at one time puffed up in display and at the next with his head high looking for the upstart on his grounds. His hens will probably be tagging along to watch the action. This can be as exciting as any confrontation with a game animal.

Challenging a gobbler is like challenging a bugling bull elk, which can result in a fighting mad animal emitting his wild, natural sounds and coming to do battle. It can stir the calmest soul. Also, it is a very effective method to lure a gobbler, as you will read in a later chapter.

The last stage in the spring behavior of the boss gobbler is when the last hen has gone to sit on her nest, not to return, and he, for the first time in many days, is alone. The first morning he wakes up and realizes the hens were not roosting with him, he usually goes crazy, spending the day running from place to place looking for them. That night he's back on the roost, hoping it was all a bad dream.

For the next few days he'll gobble a great deal both on the roost and on the ground. This is the second peak of gobbling activity. If he is an inexperienced bird he will again be "hot." In this case he will be a sucker to any hen sounds he hears and may run over the hunter in foolish abandon.

However, an older more experienced bird, although he may gobble often, uses extreme caution in his approach. And if he has become "call shy" from all the season's activity may even run from a perfectly executed, though wrong, call.

I've seen gobblers during this phase turn tail at a loud yelp. You are better off in the late season sticking to clucks and soft calls even if the old boy is gobbling up a storm. Sometimes, though, even soft calls don't work. I ran into one bird in New York state that while he was doing lots of gobbling, disappeared at the sound of any call. He did, however, respond to the sound of my careful footsteps in the leaves and my attempts to scratch in the leaves like a turkey.

Also, patience becomes a virtue because one of these old gobblers will be very wary and time-consuming in their approach. They spend many exasperating minutes standing absolutely still, head erect, observing every inch of the woods before taking another step or going into a strut. But there are enough inexperienced gobblers and enough experienced hunters around to make this the second most productive time for taking gobblers.

Chapter 10

STRATEGY FOR TAKING JAKES

Once jakes and non-dominant mature birds are ostracized from the flock and the company of hens, they seek a territory nearby where they can keep an eye on things but are out of harm's way. They often stay with other sub-dominant males. In the East it is common to see them, particularly the jakes, in pairs, though I have seen groups of five or six. In the West they are commonly in groups of six to ten or more. On the roost they gobble back at dominant birds and each other. On the ground they gobble back at the boss turkey but usually stay well away.

When the boss gobbler is in one of his gobbling moods, we hear a lot of other gobbling—his and subordinate toms—the woods seems full of turkeys. When the boss is in one of his quiet moods it seems to rub off for some reason on the others and they are also quiet and all the turkeys seem to disappear. I don't know why this is, but it sure can put a damper on things. However, let the old gobbler get shot and in a few days others start to open up. For this reason, you might venture into an area that had little gobbling other than that of a dominant bird, but after that bird is killed, gobbling may be more conspicuous than before.

Jakes and non-dominant birds can be called in, however, even if the dominant bird is still around. Some, usually a pair with a competitive nature, will come in anyway and make a rapid try to get to the hens, particularly if the old bird is spending a lot of time strutting in full display. Others will not come in until convinced the old boy is not around. If a lot of hen talk is taking place, with no sound of the gobbler, they will usually sneak in until close enough to be sure they don't see him, at which time they may race to the caller on a dead run.

When calling to jakes, don't be conservative, use a lot of calling and keep it up. If you let up they seem to lose interest except in some instances when you go completely quiet as will be mentioned in a moment. Use your cackle on them; unlike older birds they are suckers for the cackle at any time of the day.

One example of this took place here in the East; another, in the West.

One Vermont spring morning a hunting buddy, Casey Rowley, and I had just stepped out of our car at the foot of a mountain when we heard one gobble after another above us. I had killed my turkey the previous morning and now we were going after his. "Jakes" we both whispered in unison, donning our gear. We climbed an old logging road that scaled the mountain and finally worked out on a ledge above the gobbling jakes. It looked a little steep for their approach and for a while proved so. As I yelped and clucked, the jakes walked back and forth underneath us gobbling all the while. We decided to quietly move down underneath at one end when we heard them gobble at the other end. I motioned to Casey that before we moved I had one more thing to try. I cackled on my Imitator tube call and with that the gobbles changed to excited yelps and clucks. Right up the ledge they came. When they appeared over the top there were five of them and when Casey regained his composure he killed the nearest.

In another situation, we were driving along a Western canyon when we came around a corner and spotted six jakes moving under the rimrock. For the heck of it, I drove farther up the canyon and when around the bend left the truck and climbed the canyon wall to intercept them. It proved a more difficult climb than expected. When I got to where I planned to wait, I saw they were already past and above me. There was no place to hide without too much movement so I just lay on my stomach and made a cackle on a Perfection Double D mouth diaphragm. Immediately the line of jakes became a frontal assault which only stopped when I raised my gun barrel to ward them off.

In both cases the jakes had little reason to think an old gobbler was around, so their reaction was instantaneous and their competitive urge made them extremely aggressive.

Conversely, if jakes think the boss is around they will not act that quickly. It may take more doing to start them in.

One spring I knew a nice gobbler roosted with his hens in a pine stand

Pre-hunt planning is important even for an experienced hunter. Check with local game personnel about best chances of getting into good turkey habitat.

and strutted in the corner of a meadow below the stand. Opening morning before dawn I left the car and soon heard what I thought was the gobbler in a large maple above the pine stand. Answering his gobble was an obvious jake in another hardwood about 100 yards away. I set-up below the big maple and waited for fly-down time. Just as it got light I heard a now unmistakable single old bird gobble in the pines. I had set-up under a jake who just learned to gobble a little better and it was too late to change. I called anyway but was too far away to compete with the hens so I had to put off the thought of taking the old gobbler until another day.

There was no point in wasting the morning. I hauled out my pocket camera and decided to have some fun. For a long time my calling got plenty of gobbles from the jake above me, each gobble followed by one from the other jake. I kept up a steady series of clucks, yelps, and cackles. Finally, the jake decided there was too much going on without any obvious response from the old gobbler and he came half strutting and gobbling down through the woods. I got to my knees to take pictures, but apparently, when fully outlined with nothing breaking up my shape, I did not look like a boss gobbler to him so he kept coming. He was close enough to get with my 35mm, semi-wide angle lens, and as long as I kept talking he stuck around. When he heard the film advance he would deflate and start away but more calling would bring him back. As long as he did not see a threatening adversary he did not mind me. He must have had the upper hand on the other jake for during this activity all the other did was answer gobble for gobble.

Another thing to remember when dealing with jake pairs is their lesser fear of a shotgun blast. If one goes down the other may show some sign of alarm and putt, but if the hunter answers the putt with putts of his own and continues with softer clucks, the second jake can be called back. Remember this in areas where two birds in one day are legal or where two hunters are involved and you both understand that nobody moves after the shot. If there is any chance the first bird is not dead, however, don't chance his recovery.

When working on only one gobbling jake that refuses to come in, presumably because he is afraid of the local gobbler, but who hangs around answering, sometimes the trick is to become silent. First, try plenty of calls. But if this doesn't work, stop all calling, as if the hen just took off. Don't be tempted to answer no matter how much he gobbles. After a while he may come over to see where everybody went.

Jakes are gregarious in the spring. They like to run together and for this reason will go to another jake.

Learning to use the "lost" call on your friction or raspy mouth call can be productive. This call often brings answers from mature gobblers too. The lost call sounds something like a mother hen making her assembly call. The jake makes a long series of coarse yelps, but slower in tempo than a mother hen, and throws in some sharp clucks. Make sure you use a coarse and raspy call or you may call in a young hen (particularly if using this call in the fall). Jakes usually answer with similar yelps or come running in, clucking. You can use this call long, loud and often without spooking birds.

You can also use it as you cover ground trying to locate a gobbler and you may not only get a jake to yelp back but you might just egg a territorial gobble out of a silent dominant bird. If a jake answers, use the call again, then switch to clucks or copy the answering bird. More often than not, the jakes will come in so quickly you will hardly have time to get ready, so remember to be in a place where you can set-up quickly before trying the call.

Do not try the "lost" call if you have just tried your hen calls. In other words, don't mix calling methods. If you worked a ridge unsuccessfully

Decoys can be especially effective for hunting jakes. The younger birds are eager to approach un-attached hens, and they have the natural curiosity of youth.

with hen talk you might try lost jake talk on the way back. Calling lost is effective both spring and fall.

Another idiosyncrasy of jakes is their love of gobbling at a raucous crow. This is not only handy in locating jakes at any time of day but if the call is made with enough rasp and pizzaz it will make jakes gobble when real crows can not. Choose a loud raspy call rather than a more subtle one designed just for calling crows. And put your lungs into it. Sometimes when you start jakes with your hen calls and they sneak in quietly to check it out, you can learn their location and progress by using your crow call.

Jakes are both hard and easy to bring in, but in either case if you try these various methods you can have a lot of fun with them.

Chapter 11

HUNTING EASTERN BIRDS

Eastern turkeys are often the most elusive to hunt. The only way you can be successful is to keep hunting a given gobbler until you either know enough about him to score or just plain luck out.

This can be a wonderful experience and I enjoy it far better than trying a different bird each day. One thing must be considered, however. If you have to skip a day or two someone else may take him and you may be wasting your time on a ghost. Occasionally you are lucky enough to find a gobbler in a place where, for one reason or another, nobody else would think of hunting, as was the case in the following story which I wrote shortly after a 1979 hunt for a New York Eastern gobbler which I call *The Chronicle of Tip Tyler's Turkey:*

The climb up the steep ridge was difficult. Our pants, soaked by the rain-drenched brush below, bound our every step. Casey Rowley and I stumbled in the darkness. But stopping for a gulp of the early morning air, discomfort was forgotten when we heard that unmistakable gobble. We grinned at each other, gritted our teeth, and resumed the upward struggle. Casey and I had one last chance, and a tight schedule to keep. This was an appointment that wouldn't wait. As a matter of fact, it would be my fifth attempt to outwit this wily old tom and the New York spring season would end in two days.

This particular wild turkey was introduced to me on a scouting trip prior to the season's opening when I stopped at a sporting goods store for information. The first step in successful turkey hunting is finding where they are. You either find them yourself or get your information second hand.

A lovely state for hunting the Eastern wild turkey, Vermont offers abundant opportunities for taking trophies.

The store owner wasn't in, but his right hand man, Tip Tyler, was there. When I asked for leads on where nearby gobblers had been observed lately, Tip allowed as how he would tell me about the biggest turkey he had ever seen.

Well, it seems this turkey grew enormous on a beautiful ridge all to himself overlooking rich fields of corn. Between him and the world was a good sized brook no one could cross and another ridge behind his was posted. The last time Tip saw the bird, his dragging wings were plowing deep furrows in a corn field as 12 lovely hens looked on in awe.

The location was pinpointed and I decided to have a look. It was just about the way he said it would be. A blacktop road ran parallel to the long main ridge and between this and the road lay the brook wandering along the ridge base and occasionally out into the lush meadows and corn fields. By the time the brook was bridged around the ends of the ridge it was well into posted land. Believing nobody else would bother the bird, a situation devoutly to be desired, I decided to keep him for myself.

Opening morning my responsibility was with visiting dignitaries who required some help finding turkeys, but with luck the two I guided scored quickly with nice yearling gobblers. As one was Rob Keck, former world champion caller, I was anxious to see if he could get a response from Tip's and my bird.

A turkey may be made to answer certain sounds and therefore give away his position. This is usually done at dusk or pre-dawn by hooting like an owl or gobbling with a turkey call made for that purpose. And sometimes it can be done during daylight hours.

We stopped along the highway opposite the center of the ridge and when all was quiet, Rob let out with an exaggerated crow call. A muffled gobble resounded from the ridge and Rob turned to me, winked, and said, "That sounded like a real good-un." Several more attempts were made to get the bird to sound off again so as to pinpoint this location, but he wasn't going to cooperate. We decided to go over and give him a try anyway.

After gathering our gear, we crossed the fields and looked for an easy place to cross the brook. There wasn't any. A farmer could stay high and dry fording the brook with his tractor, but we went over our boot tops as we tried to hop across. Traveling slowly and quietly we crossed a pine knoll and came to the edge of a small meadow at the base of the main ridge. This looked like the only place open enough to try luring our turkey. We got set and Rob put his ample bag of tricks to work. There was no answer from the bird, but I had a fantastic lesson in calling which I greatly appreciated. We then walked along the brook, looking for a better crossing, but in the end got just as wet on the way back.

My hunting continued in Vermont during the next several days and a nice Jake fell to my efforts. Now I wanted a long beard. It was time to cross the brook again and try my special turkey.

The first day we returned, Niles Oesterle, newly elected president of the

Vermont State Chapter of the National Wild Turkey Federation, old friend, and top-notch caller, was my hunting companion. Niles had three days off and a three day New York license. This was his second day. However, this time even though we were able to get the old gobbler to respond each time we called from the road, first on his roost and later seemingly from the meadow, we found no sign of him when we reached the ridge.

The next morning we got his answer again from the roost as we called from the roadside. This time we hot-footed it across the brook and up to the meadow where we assumed he would fly down as he had the day before. We got into position as quietly and as quickly as possible and attempted once more to lure him, first with soft clucks and tree yelps and later with our full repertoire. No luck. We gave up and just before leaving Niles tried some very loud high pitched yelps and "cutts" as he stood in the middle of the meadow. Was that a gobble? It had worked. He tried again and our bird answered from the top of the ridge.

Now if you have never pursued a turkey when the woods are fully leafed, you haven't missed a thing. Between the lack of visibility and the muffling effect of the underbrush and overhead canopy, it is all but impossible to figure out just how far away the bird is, even when you get him to answer you. We labored our way slowly up the ridge alternately slipping and sliding on the wet, shaley soil and then finding decent places to hide each time we called to him to keep in touch. By the time we reached the top, Niles and I were about 100 yards apart.

The last time the turkey gobbled he was to my left, Niles was to my right. Crawling on my hands and knees, I was looking for easy going and a place to hide when Niles opened up with his call. The turkey answered and was not far away.

I sank to my belly. Niles was giving him the works and getting results. Suddenly I could see the head of the big bird as he moved through some hardwood saplings at not more than 40 yards. I was tempted to take a shot, but Niles was working the bird and the bird was definitely heading for him.

Even if he was my private bird, this was Nile's last day, and, well, I just couldn't do it. At least I'd finally seen the old boy and that was a thrill in itself.

As the turkey went by and out of sight I worked my way around by an old log to wait in case he decided to come back. I had to make myself comfortable several times in the next two hours that Niles kept conversing with the bird. The old Tom was hot, rattling out his unmistakable gobble every time Niles gave him a series of yelps or a cackle. It was a great thing to hear and I wouldn't have minded listening all day. Niles has been referred to as the best amateur caller in the Northeast and this old bird was no amateur.

In spite of his obvious excitement, the Tom would not leave his gobbling ground, but continuously moved back and forth within it. Our portion at the top of the ridge was an open park-like area of short grass with an occasional big hardwood and patches of small hardwood saplings. It was a beautiful spot for either man or beast, and the bird knew it well.

Suddenly, after a particularly hot round of exchanges, I was startled by the sound of Niles' shot. After making sure that a missed or crippled bird was not heading in my direction, I ran to the scene of the hunt. Niles was frantically searching for a downed bird as he kept up a steady, unfathomable mutter.

He quieted down long enough to tell his story and show me where the bird was when he shot at it. This was verified by finding some shot in a nearby tree. Then while I stood there he went to his hiding place from which he had fired. As he reached the top of a little knoll, I realized there would be no dead bird. After all that calling and excitement, the old gobbler had finally shown himself and this was too much for my frustrated friend. Without thinking he shot from about 80 yards. Even a buffered, plated, 3-inch magnum load will not kill one of these tough old critters at that range.

We left the ridge dejected and what's more, as we did, a Jake continued to gobble on the back side of the ridge and, according to Niles, he had been doing this all the while—but our hunting time had run out.

It was over for Niles, but not for me. I was convinced that old gobbler was not hurt and would be at it again. I now knew that he roosted in one of the big oaks on the side of the ridge, flew down in the morning to the little meadow, and then quickly made his way up to the park-like area on the top where he would hold forth in hopes of luring in one of those hens that somehow escaped his earlier advances. And I also now knew how best to approach his strutting ground.

I gave the turkey a few day's rest, then convinced an old hunting buddy, Casey Rowley, to go with me on the understanding that the bird was mine. I would do the calling, but there would also be the Jake to attend to. Now Casey and I have hunted together for years, everything from caribou in the Ungava to geese on the Eastern Shore and for some unknown reason we have never failed to have a good time.

Earlier heavy spring rains had swollen our brook to a waist deep torrent, but Niles and I had crossed each day in waders carrying over our boots and gear. Casey didn't have any waders. He stripped down to bare skin and simply waded the river, then climbed back into his clothes and boots on the other side.

We hadn't even tied our boots when we heard the now unmistakable challenge from the tree. We worked our way carefully up the ridge and after a couple more gobbles from the roost, we heard the muffled gobble from down in the meadow. We didn't have much time now for those powerful legs would take the turkey up the ridge far faster than those of a mere man.

I got into a good place somewhere in between where Niles and I were two days before and sent Casey on toward where Niles had been, and unenthusiastically told him, "Take a shot if you get one."

It wasn't long before a gobble rattled out up on top, a short way in the direction from which we had come. I started first with soft clucks and purrs with no response. Remember, sounds don't travel as well as when the trees are bare. Louder yelps did the trick. Then he never let the conversation end. Sometimes sounding so close that I strained to see him sometimes back at a distance where I wondered if he could hear me, but always he answered my notes. When I cackled, he double and triple gobbled. Now, as two days before, this went on and on. (With more experience gained since this hunt I have learned more about using the cackle.) I tried being quiet for a while and then in nervous impatience would call again only to be answered in the same way. I tried cackling without stopping as he gobbled every time I took a breath between calls and then started gobbling at the rat-a-tat-tat-tat of a nearby woodpecker. But he came no nearer.

I'm a great believer in moving on a bird, if necessary. And now was the time in spite of the fact that it was almost impossible to tell exactly where he was. I dropped down the back of the ridge and circled to go into the area that I thought was the far end of his strutting ground. There I found an old tree stub that looked out on a likely area for him to move into.

I called again and got the usual reply. I waited for a while, called again and got the same results. Having gotten away with it once, I tried to move closer. No sooner had I found an upturned stump to hide under, than a gobble resounded not 50 yards away. Looking uphill I raised my gun as I

A successful hunter packs his bird out of typical Eastern habitat.

actually heard him moving through the open grass. He was there running for my last position. In that instant, before I could think to bring gun to cheek and fire, he saw me and was gone. Casey, who had taken my grandstand seat of two days earlier, was less kind than I was when in his position. He berated me and derided me about how I handled the whole affair. However, the ground work was laid for the following morning.

With the gobbler's greeting from his roost that morning, our plans and the opportunity to amend our previous mistakes were to be given another chance. In a few moments I had taken my spot beside an old fallen log somewhere in the middle of his range.

Casey was somewhere up the ridge. Now was the time to cool off from our rapid ascent and tune in to the marvelous sounds and sights of the breaking dawn. First, as light approaches, places in the woods that had looked so far off now are only a few yards away. The quiet becomes full of noises. The ground and tree tops become full of activity. A very small mouse conducting his normal journey under the protection of the log made a detour over my elbow, and birds of all kinds began mating rituals around me.

The tempo of my heartbeat suddenly changed because of another sound. When the old tom first hit the top he gobbled just about where I had expected him to. I decided to do two things. First, make sure he answered me and then, this time, to be quiet and wait him out.

Lying along the downhill side of the log, my various calls were handy to my right hand, and a diaphragm call was in my mouth. My gun was across my stomach and legs where I could bring it to quick command of the open grassy area in the hardwoods to my left below me. The turkey should either show up at my feet or off my left side according to all I had learned from our previous hunts. Just above and to my right were some thick berry bushes through which he was not likely to approach. Farther to my right on the other side of the log were some more small hardwood saplings, but this was an area that I had not been able to call the turkey through the day previous. I was well satisfied with my choice as the turkey responded to my initial calls.

I yelped. With his answer I gave my best cackle and shut up. To my dismay, after the silence following, I heard him gobble as he approached in the saplings to my right.

Turkey hunters and layout shooters are keenly aware of the frustration that comes from birds arriving on the side of your shooting hand.

The tom continued to gobble as he approached from my bad side. I squirmed around behind the log to better my chances. Just when I figured he would get past me, I ventured a soft cluck on my mouth diaphragm. I did so out of desperation, because I have little faith in the cluck with this instrument.

But this time for some unknown reason, even I knew it had worked. My shotgun barrel now stuck over the log in plain sight. I figured my chance of seeing the turkey before he saw me was ridiculous.

Then a great black chest and beard appeared—how to get my gun to bear? There was no faltering in his step and he kept coming. He came to a stump, not large enough under normal circumstances, but from my near prone position, might just hide me from him as he passed. As he stepped clear I made sure that I was looking down that rib as if it were a match target rifle and his neck was my 10 ring. With the shot he was down. It was all over. Not even the usual flop to misplace any feathers. He lay in all his glory and once more I had all those crazy feelings that come from such a hunt.

The bond that develops between hunter and quarry when this type of relationship arises and that necessary anticlimax that finishes it was there. He lay in the grass, early sun rays bouncing copper, gold, and green off his feathers and his beard stretching nearly 11 inches long. His weight turned out to be 18 pounds, a bit below the estimates given me by Tip Tyler. But who knows, a month of breeding and then almost a month of hoping (it was now June 1) and all this time scarcely eating, would raise hell with a corpulent figure. More importantly, however, as I embraced Rowley, was the culmination of an experience hard to impress upon the uniniated who haven't yet hunted the wild turkey.

Turkey hunting cannot always be done close to home and in an exclusive area or over several days without interruption as occurred with Tip Tyler's turkey.

When the hunter finds himself in a new part of the country with limited time to hunt he may be forced to do his hunting on public grounds. My first two hunts for the Florida turkey were spent in the Three Lakes Wildlife Management Area in south Florida near Kenansville. This area encompasses 42,000 acres and parts of lakes Jackson, Marian, and Kissimmee. Along with your Florida hunting license you must also purchase a management area permit and check in and out of the area you hunt. Maps are available showing all roads which are numbered or marked. Some of these roads are no more than wheel tracks in sandy soil and I missed one night's roosting opportunity dragging my rental car out of the sand on one of these stretches. However, the sandy soil does allow the hunter to look for and identify fresh turkey tracks.

Late one afternoon I found two sets of gobbler tracks crossing a road and made within the hour. The tracks were headed into a freshly burned over palmetto flat growing grass for cattle and containing a few scattered pines. About 500 yards ahead in the direction of the tracks was a large Cypress head and a smaller one lay off to the right another 300 yards away. I assumed the gobblers were going for the large head to roost and therefore I was back in the area before dawn the next morning.

I picked my way in the dark across the burn and looked for a suitable place to set-up without crowding the Cypress swamp. With no trees big enough to conceal me, I backed into a thick palmetto bush facing the roost. Just before daylight I heard a gobble in the head in front of me and an answering gobble in the other head off to the right. I clucked in response and all was quiet.

I kept waiting for the gobbler in front of me to show up. After a while I cackled once and then maintained my vigil. Now, these management area birds have had a bit of experience. As a matter of fact, that opening weekend there were 500 hunters who checked in and out of Three Lakes Area and their kill for the weekend was three gobblers.

It would have been four, if I hadn't goofed. I sat absolutely still, moving only my eyes, searching for the silent gobbler I hoped was sneaking up in front of me. Then I saw movement. Turning my head slowly to the right, I found myself eye-to-eye with a gobbler just the other side of the palmetto.

For some reason the far gobbler was the one to come in. I remembered a story Dave Harbour told me about his son being caught in the same situation.

When Dave's son slowly lowered his box call to the ground in order to get ready to shoot, the box call made a squawk as it landed, the gobbler immediately went into a strut. Dave's son got the chance to shoot.

But my gobbler was not that kind. Instead he looked a little sheepish and slowly stole out of sight behind another smaller bush. I jumped to my feet getting ready to shoot, but he had just disappeared—they will do that.

Florida gobblers on public grounds get a lot of pressure. They become very call-shy and silent. More often they can be roosted by the sound of them flying up, rather than by gobbling. And often you will hear them fly down rather than hear an early morning gobble. If you run into this situation you had better limit your calling to a few clucks with lots of time between calls. They have heard everything else and can be hard to come by.

After you get over your fear of snakes and 'gators (many snakes are nocturnal, take a good flashlight), and you get used to the chiggers and turkeys that run and feed in water and don't talk much, you might be lucky enough to bag one and it will be worth it I promise. I have one mounted in my office with a 1⅜-inch spur, a dandy beard, and a stream-lined body that glows with an iridescent beauty beyond comparison.

Chapter 12
HUNTING WESTERN BIRDS

Hunting Western turkeys the first time for an Eastern turkey hunter can be quite an experience. The Rio Grande turkey of the Southwest likes habitat far different from either of our Eastern birds. My first introduction to Rio Grandes was like my first mule deer hunt.

I was stationed at Denver and for my first mule deer hunt I chose an area in central Colorado. In those days it was a multiple deer area which meant you could take as many mule deer as you were willing to buy licenses for. Figuring this meant there were too many deer in the area, and being an experienced Eastern whitetail hunter, I figured this was a piece of cake.

I scouted around but found no typical deer cover. The hillsides were nothing but grass and sagebrush. I finally found a wooded draw leading from one hill to another and assumed any deer in its right mind would follow this cover. Opening morning, before dawn, I parked myself atop the draw and waited. At daylight I heard shots all around me. But nothing stirred in the draw. I finally ventured out to see what was going on. To my amazement, hunters were not shooting jackrabbits out in the open sage but were killing mule deer.

Rio Grandes are the mule deer of the turkey family. The stories of two Rio Grande hunts will demonstrate what I mean.

I was hunting the Black Kettle National Grasslands in Roger Mills County, Oklahoma which is managed by Bill McCaslan, game biologist for the state. I had a Forest Service map (which is available to anyone) of the Black Kettle area showing public and private land as well as roads and water courses. The latter were vitally important because often the only timber capable of roosting turkeys is found along these creeks.

It is also very important to know which quarter sections are public

Hunting Western birds can provide added excitement in the beauty of the terrain and the bird it-self. Techniques differ from those used in other parts of the country. Here, Paul Bruun ap-proaches his Merriam turkey.

grassland and which are private. Posting is only required at corners and access points if the land is fenced, and you don't want to hunt on private ground anywhere in the West without permission.

Bill was good enough to mark my map as to where turkeys had been sighted. Trees were scarce and with the exception of some patches of scrub oak and other trees of that size the only decent roosting areas were the cottonwoods along drainages and creeks. Because of this, as mentioned before, the Rio Grande is very limited in his choice of roost sites. And for this reason it is against the law in Oklahoma to shoot a turkey on the roost. There is a lot of deep-well natural gas production in Roger Mills County and we found birds roosting in cottonwoods next to drilling rigs whose gigantic diesels howled around the clock.

I constantly looked for some kind of cover leading from roosting sites into other areas such as patches of scrub oak where I assumed the turkeys would feed and loaf. I did find scratchings in small patches of oak.

My first exposure to the cover these birds prefer came as I worked through a patch of mixed woods. Stopping to make a series of yelps on my Neil Cost box call, I heard a faint answer. I moved in that direction and soon came to the edge of a grassy area stretching for half a mile down toward a creek bottom. I assumed the gobble came from the creek bottom—which was the only other place as far as the eye could see with any trees or cover.

Walking along the edge of the woods, I found an erosion gully I assumed would allow me to sneak down to the creek. I made another series of yelps before starting in order to pinpoint the gobbler. I got an answer and it sounded much closer but that seemed impossible so I assumed it was just the wind carrying the sound. I hadn't gone very far down the gully when I thought I heard a cluck.

I peaked over the top and there right out in the middle of all that grass was a mature Rio Grande gobbler, which upon spying me was off and running. He wasn't following the gully or any form of cover I was familiar with.

I mentioned this to Bill McCaslan and he laughed and said, "It's normal for birds to spend all day out in the open grassland."

But some habits are hard to break and I made the same mistake again. This time I roosted a gobbler across a field from where I found a lot of sign in some scrub oak patches, and around a water tank for cattle fed by a pumping windmill.

A fence led directly from the roost area to the oak patches and there were just enough trees and brush along this fence to supply the kind of cover an eastern bird would use to cross the opening. Before dawn the next morning I followed the fence into the roosting area.

When I got there the trees were hardly 10 feet high, so I continued on, looking for larger, potential roosting trees to set-up near. I hadn't taken many steps when I flushed a turkey, barely six feet off the ground, from a tree. I quickly back tracked and found a little pile of brush to sit against right on the fence. If I hadn't scared the turkeys I figured I had it made if they were to head for the oaks and water.

After a bit I heard birds fly down so I started calling. It was obvious there were a lot of turkeys there. Soon I had two jakes looking me over, but I was hoping for a chance at a mature gobbler. I let them come almost into my lap then quit calling so as not to spook them.

After they left I raised my head to look around and there, out in the middle of the open grass, was a half strutting, half running gobbler along with a couple of jakes tagging along after 15 hens headed for the water tank. For the second time I was fooled by a turkey who prefers wide open spaces. It is said that a scared Eastern turkey runs to the woods, while a scared Rio Grande turkey runs to the open fields.

Merriam's turkeys like open country too, but certainly not like Rio Grandes. Timber and cover are plentiful in Merriam's habitat. The birds also have plenty of places to roost but tend to use the same spot often. The Black Hills of South Dakota and Wyoming, although not original Merriam's range, are ideal for them and could be considered typical habitat. Merriam's were introduced to the Black Hills about 30 years ago and now this may be the largest concentration of them in the West. It is also one of the largest areas of public hunting, so big in fact that turkey hunters tap only a small portion of it.

The Black Hills National forest covers a very large area west of Rapid City, South Dakota and spills into a smaller area of Wyoming east and north of Newcastle and reaches to the base of Devil's Tower. Turkeys may be hunted from sunrise to sunset in both Wyoming and South Dakota. Currently, in South Dakota, non-residents pay $2 for a general hunting license and an additional $10 for a turkey stamp. This is the best bargain anywhere. Wyoming, even though there is no need of it as far as turkey numbers are concerned, uses a limited lottery with application deadlines in mid-winter.

An excellent large scale and detailed map of the Black Hills National Forest is available from the Forest Service. A Black Hills turkey hunt, or almost any Merriam's hunt, be it in Colorado, New Mexico, or Arizona, takes place in some of the wildest, most beautiful habitat. The Merriam's share their canyons, Ponderosa pine, and rim-rock with whitetails, mule deer, elk, bear, and mountain lion as well as coyotes and other creatures.

In one canyon I hunted, we spooked a small herd of elk almost every morning. One day we met them as we rounded a bend. As they ran up a steep game trail, they passed a turkey coming down. The poor bird was left spinning around in bewilderment.

It is a beautiful and rugged country and by the same token the hunting can be tough. If you are planning a Western elk hunt on foot you can start getting in shape with a Merriam's turkey hunt. Any one who can catch up

Ben Conger checks turkey tracks in the Black Hills of Wyoming.

to or get ahead of Merriam's on the move is in good enough shape to take on anything. The best tactic I've found is to figure out their daily pattern, get ahead of them and wait for them to arrive.

A group of Merriam's was roosting in a short side canyon and they were there so often that we named it "roosting canyon." Their pattern was to fly from the roost to the top of the main canyon, walk to the rim-rock, then some would fly across the main canyon (most of the hens) while others, along with the old gobbler, walked down. There they would take a quick drink in the creek and walk across and up the other side.

I found a little clearing about 100 yards up the far side which looked perfect for some early morning strutting. I climbed to the clearing at dawn and as I approached it I heard hens that had already flown across. Quickly, I set-up against a thick juniper at the bottom of the clearing, with my left shoulder to the open area. Soon, hens were yelping all around me.

I did some yelping also, trying to sound just a little more excited than the others. All of a sudden, around the juniper right at my feet, came a couple of hens. I didn't move as they picked their way across the clearing. Then I could hear the whuff, whuff, of dragging wings and, peeking through the branches, I saw a magnificant gobbler, also about to arrive at my feet.

There was no way I could get the gun up without being seen; he was too close anyway, unless I wanted to club him. Just moving my eyeballs I watched him strut by and decided to let him get away from me and when his back was to me, tail up hiding his head, I could get my gun up to shoot. Then the moment finally came when out of the corner of my eye I saw the tail fan out. I turned. As I started to move the gun, to my dismay, I saw he was facing me from 10 feet away. I tried out drawing him, but by the time I was ready to fire I could no longer see his head and gave up the shot.

Trying to get your gun on a turkey that has spotted you is almost impossible. Do not attempt it because the shot it may give will seldom be a killing head shot. (A friend of mine claims he can immobilize a turkey at a time like this by cackling with his mouth call as he brings his gun up. I can't vouch for this as I've never had the presence of mind to try it.)

I knew I'd have another chance the next morning so I looked the clearing over to pick a better spot to set-up. I was there a little earlier and sat at the base of an uprooted pine near the top of the clearing. I looked down into the entire area containing the junipers. To my right, however, was a rock outcropping that hid some of the area from me.

The hens arrived as before and I heard the old boy gobbling. Again, amid the hen chorus, I tried excited yelps on my box. The tom gobbled at my yelps so I knew I'd get a shot. I switched to a Perfection Double D mouth call and made some very soft chirping yelps. Soon I heard the whuff, whuff, of his wing tips only now it was coming from the other side of the rock outcropping. Was I going to have him in my lap again? I steadied my gun across my knees aiming for the point on the rimrock above the sound. Then just like a sun rise, those white tail tips appeared giving me time to home-in before the old, warty white head showed. All I saw was head and tail when I fired.

I don't know if he was downed by shot or rock shrapnel but he was very dead when I got to him.

I hung around, waiting for enough sun to take pictures. I was never happier, sitting beside this beautiful bird. Black iridescent feathers contrasted with creamy white rump and tail feather tips. His hook-shaped spurs turned black as they tapered to a point over 1-inch-long, a thick brush of bristle formed a beard over 9-inches-long. Even his warty old head was handsome.

What great country in which to enjoy the grand spring hunt.

Chapter 13

PUTTING IT ALL TOGETHER

After you have hunted all four sub-species with a fair degree of success in different years, what do you do for an encore? I found myself in Florida on a late spring afternoon with just such a thought running through my mind. But the answer would have to wait. Right now I needed to blow my crow call. At the squawk of the crow call, a gobbler answered from over near the swamp. Then a second gobble sounded from down the treeline. I decided, while heading back to camp in the twilight, to try for the swamp bird.

The next morning, before dawn, I crossed a burned area with cow paths glowing in the moonlight. Then I hit heavy brush and blundered into a fence.

This bird is having nightmares by now, I thought to myself. So, I backed away from the fence and edged over to a little clearing, hoping the gobbler might fly down into it. As it grew lighter, I began making little circles in the center of my slate, producing tree yelps. A gobble roared back from overhead. He was in a pine tree on the swamp's edge only a few yards away.

Another scratch on the slate was answered by another gobble. I heard, then saw, him fly down. He gobbled several times after landing off to my left.

He answered my clucks, but he wasn't coming in. Obviously, he heard or saw me.

Bart Jacob's Florida Grand Slam bird.

I'll get him tomorrow, I thought to myself, if he's in the same area. And he should be because he wasn't that frightened.

The idea of getting an Osceola gobbler began the year before, but I couldn't arrange for the time. Luckily, this spring I was invited to hunt with Dave Harbour, immediately after the National Wild Turkey Federation Convention.

When I arrived at Lake Marian in Florida, Dave and a fellow he was guiding told me they heard turkeys talking while they were out bass fishing. We went to where they heard the birds and roosted two gobblers, using the crow call. Now it was early morning and my gobbler was gone. It flew in Dave's direction.

Avoiding that area, I prowled the swamp edge. An hour later, not hearing shots or calling from Dave's direction, I went looking for him.

"I didn't see nor hear a bird," Dave said when we met. After hearing my story Dave and his client decided to hunt a different area, and we agreed to meet at one o'clock.

This bird is mine, I thought to myself, back at the swamp edge. Then I went to the roost tree and studied the area. I walked the gobbler's flight path and found a little clearing. Tracks indicated it was the gobbler's fly-down area. The bushes looked dense in the area. However, near the ground you could see clearly. "This is where I'll be tomorrow morning," I told myself, while scouting a clear approach to the fly down area. With my plans made I went woods wandering. Around 10 a.m. I found myself back at the fly down area again. I scratched out a yelp on my slate, not really expecting an answer, but a gobble roared back. I froze, then quickly backed into a thick bush and sat down. I roughed up my slate and popped a few clucks on it. A gobble from half the distance of the first one came back. Shortly, the gobbler appeared, coming through the brush. When he slid behind a bush, I mounted the gun to my shoulder. He dropped 30 paces away.

He looked like he had only a short beard while coming through the brush which meant he was a jake. But as I approached him I saw huge spurs sticking out. Up close, even his beard looked good. It measured nine inches.

After congratulating myself, I slung the bird over my shoulder and headed out. Dave was napping in his 4WD. I put the bird on the tailgate and woke him.

"Oh geez," Dave squealed, "look at those spurs. He's a dandy." (This bird was number 17 with the longest spurs and number 24 overall in The First World Record Book.)

You know how praise fires you up. Dave's praise had me strutting like a gobbler. "Geez," I said, "I can get a Merriam's, I'm pretty sure." And Dave said, "Why not go for the turkey grand slam."

That was the beginning of the grand slam idea.

Returning to Vermont, I called Don Valentine, my Wyoming buddy. He offered transportation via his airplane for my try for both the Merriam's and Rio Grande birds.

Don agreed to arrange the Wyoming hunt; I, the Oklahoma hunt. I arranged for a guide in Oklahoma, but a week before we were to leave, the guide hurt his back. In desperation, I telephoned Bill McCaslan, State Biologist for the Black Kettle National Grassland Area and the Northwest Central part of Oklahoma, except for the panhandle.

Bill said he would help us. Since the area he suggested was public land, there was no problem obtaining permission to hunt. The grand slam was back on track.

Don met me at the Denver airport and we agreed to hunt Wyoming first.

We left Denver with the weather report calling for scattered squalls. But a solid front came through. At Lusk, Wyoming, we could see no way around the deteriorating weather so we landed there in a driving rain. We were 80 miles from Newcastle, our destination. After securing the airplane, we called Don's partner, Paul, in Newcastle and he agreed to drive down and pick us up.

We arrived in camp after midnight. It was raining hard. Four hours later I crawled out of the sack. Rain still pounded on the cabin roof. I ached mentally and physically. I had five days to score in both Wyoming and Oklahoma. Foul weather wasn't in my plans. I went hunting in spite of the weather which was snow mixed with rain driven by high winds.

I went to a spot where I'd killed a gobbler a few years ago. There was no roost talk. Nothing. A bird 50 feet away couldn't be heard in such a storm.

Just after daylight I saw Don coming up through the canyon with the pickup truck, and I walked over and intercepted him. I was cold, wet and miserable. It was stupid to be out on such a day.

When we returned to camp, Paul was gone. We figured he went hunting up on the rimrock near camp. We went looking for him in the pickup truck. We found him walking down the road with a huge gobbler on his shoulder.

By now small patches of blue were appearing on the western horizon behind the storm. We drove to Newcastle and Don got a buddy to fly him to Lusk for his airplane.

Paul and I drove back to camp and he took me up to where he shot his bird. I decided to show Paul my new "1-Hander" slate call. I clucked. A hen raced in. Hearing nothing else, we walked back to the truck and drove on.

A little farther on I said, "Why don't I try one more call?"

We stopped. I got out and let out a series of yelps. Paul said, "I think I heard something."

So I stepped around to his side, waited a few minutes and yelped again. A gobbler answered.

I ran through the woods and sat down behind a log, 50 yards from the truck. Then I began clucking. And this old boy ran in like a race horse. I followed him with the gun and dumped him at 20 yards. (With three beards and weighing 19½ pounds he ended up number 2 in the non typical gobbler category in the world gobbler records.) Two down and two to go.

At 9 a.m. the next morning we were in the air. Four hours later we landed at Gage, Oklahoma. Bill McCaslan met us at the airport and gave us National Grassland Maps with marked areas he recommended.

We drove out to scout some of the better looking areas. I found a line of trees along a ravine next to a railroad. They were cottonwoods mixed with hardwoods. That was where I intended to hunt.

Don and I began hunting about a mile apart the next morning.

Before dawn I crossed a small creek. While wading, I heard a gobbler on the roost ahead of me. In the darkness I got as close as I dared and seated myself on the ground in the thick, lower branches of a small evergreen with my back against its trunk.

The gobbler stayed on the roost well after daybreak. I clucked with the slate, but he gobbled so much I couldn't tell whether he was gobbling at my clucking or just gobbling at the sunrise. Then he flew down, gobbling steadily. But he was going away from me. That's when I yelped. Not getting an immediate response, I figured I had spooked him.

Then I heard him coming back. I resumed yelping. Then I clucked and purred. He kept coming. Straight ahead, I saw movement. Two jakes.

It was then that something which always puzzles me cropped up again. I can understand a turkey pinpointing the direction of a call. What amazes me is how they know the distance. There was a locust log in front of me and the two jakes couldn't come directly at me. They detoured the log and then came directly toward me. This happens to me time and time again.

Suddenly, I wasn't sure if I wanted a jake. Then I said to myself, "this is silly." The next time they separated, I shot. (This bird failed to qualify in the record book.)

The second jake ran a few steps, putting like crazy. I putted and purred on the slate and he stopped. He came back when I purred and clucked some more. This is typical of jake behavior. When I stood up he putted and ran off.

I walked out and located Don. He was birdless. If I had known how few birds were around I could have taken Don back and called the other jake in. All you have to do is act the part of his lost buddy and he will run right in. As it was, the weather got hotter, it hit 100 degrees, and it was time to go home. Don didn't get a bird and I never saw another turkey in Oklahoma either.

If I were to hunt that area again I would make sure to hit it on opening day. Or I would wait until the last two days of the season, hoping most of the birds that were spooked from public to private ground had returned. Using either method you should get a bird.

The last leg of the grand slam was to be a home bird. Opening morning in Vermont, I went to where I roosted a big gobbler the night before. By

Typical habitat in Florida, where the cover sometimes provides more than enough camouflage for the hunter.

the time I heard the old bird gobble, I had two jakes coming in. It was impossible to work the old bird without spooking the jakes. And if I spooked the jakes, they would spook the old bird. I was trapped.

Two days later, on Monday, I missed a big bird. It came in silently. All I heard were footsteps in the leaves. When he appeared, all I saw was a head peeking over a white birch log. I moved the gun muzzle a few inches and he was gone.

Day after day I tried for different birds, but something always went wrong. Then I located this big bird in Wells. There was a ravine with a corn field and road on one side. A logging road ran along the other side. The gobbler and his hens roosted in a big maple at the end of the ravine.

Every morning a hunter drove into the area in a light blue pickup. Whichever side of the ravine he drove in on the turkeys went the other way. Not knowing which direction the pickup would come from, I never knew where the birds would fly.

The Friday before the end of the season, I decided to go after the big bird in Wells, no matter what. I wasn't having any luck elsewhere.

At the end of the ravine was a knoll. I convinced myself that no matter where he started from my gobbler ended up on that knoll. I figured this out by watching his hens. Every time I was up by the knoll and a hen came by she moved like a cat. From experience, I knew a hen, who has just left a gobbler, moves only a few steps at a time, then stands perfectly still for several minutes before moving again. Finally, when far enough away, she moves normally. After watching hens do this several times up near the knoll I knew my gobbler ended up there . . . every day.

I was on that knoll long before daylight and let out a helluva fly-down cackle on my box call at first light. A gobble came from the ravine. He was still roosting in his favorite maple. Sitting against an oak, where I could look down the ravine, I waited for fly-down time. Then I scratched out a few yelps. He gobbled. It came from the maple tree area but I could tell he was on the ground. In a little while I scratched out a couple more yelps and he was much closer. I said to myself, "I got you now old buddy. I got my grand slam." There was no way he could reach the knoll without passing me. Shortly, I scratched out another yelp. No response. Nothing.

Then I heard a gobble far away. He was gone. What happened? After a few minutes I sneaked down the ravine, moving from one little cedar to another, stopping often to scratch out calls until I got to the road. There sat the blue pickup. My world collapsed. I had gotten this attitude that not only was I going to lose my grand slam in my own backyard, but I was going to be skunked for the first time in Vermont. I dreaded the riding I would take if I got skunked. I walked back up the ridge. I went up there because I knew I would have to come down through this old bird's territory in order to get back to my car.

It was about 9 a.m. when I started back down. I convinced myself to go up on the knoll one last time. But I knew my chance for a grand slam was gone. Because this particular bird had been so difficult to call with seductive yelps, and I have never done this before, I decided to challenge him. Before I crossed the barbed wire fence on the edge of the knoll, I gobbled.

And boy, right down beneath me, a gobble roared back.

I slid under a cedar and yelped seductively on the tube. No answer. Then I gobbled. He gobbled. I came right back with a gobble on the tube while scratching an aggravated purr on the slate.

He went wild. He was coming all the time, gobbling continuously. I expected to see him at anytime, so I dropped the tube and picked up my gun. But I kept up the aggravated purr on the "1-Hander."

Then I saw him. He was with two hens. He came through low brush and it became hard to see him. I sighted at his head, following him as closely as I could. Then I shifted the gun to stay on his head and the head vanished.

Oh no, I screamed to myself. Not again.

But then the head reappeared. He hadn't seen me; he was moving. Then he stepped into the clear. I hit him, at exactly 15 paces, and he rolled down the hill. I ran over, but it was a solid hit. He wasn't going anywhere.

He weighed 21 pounds. Seven tail feathers and some of his cover feathers over the tail were missing. The insides of his legs, breast and underbelly were featherless from fighting. He had only $\frac{7}{8}$-inch spurs, indicating he was probably a three-year-old. (He ended up Number 140 overall in the record book.)

The day after I killed my gobbler, Ed Connors, who owns a garage in the area, told me he saw the biggest gobbler of his life fly across the road and land in the area where I harvested mine. He figures the old boy was going back to claim his hens. I think he's right. I knew where I'd be opening day of the following gobbler season . . . sitting on that same knoll.

But I'm sure I'll never try for a gobbler grand slam in the same year again. Well, almost sure. I wonder if anyone has ever taken a grand slam with a bow and arrow?

Footnote: You can check turkey records in *Advanced Wild Turkey Hunting & World Records* by Dave Harbour and published by Winchester Press.

Chapter 14

BOWHUNTING

The hunter who purposely locates, calls, and finally harvests a mature gobbler with bow and arrow has accomplished bowhunting's ultimate challenge.

The bowhunter must first use all of the tactics we have mentioned for shotgunners. Then he must compensate for his device which is more difficult to carry in the woods, to hide, to hold, to prepare for the shot, to shoot, and to make an "on the spot" kill with. However, there are both methods and gear which can help.

The first thing the bowhunter learns is how to handle his equipment as he travels through the woods. He learns how to maneuver his bow and arrows quietly and without damaging them. The use of brush buttons on a recurve bow and just plain care with the compound bow so as not to lodge branches, etc., between cable and wheel or cam is necessary.

Arrows should be held securely in a bow quiver mounted on the bow or carried in your hand. Old fashioned back quivers with fletching sticking up where arrows catch when you bend over to sneak under branches, are noisy and annoying. I have fashioned a back quiver utilizing a bow quiver where the arrows are held securely, fletching down and nothing sticks up to catch when I bend over. I can take it off in a moment when I am ready to set up.

There is never a need to carry an arrow nocked on the string when bowhunting turkeys. If you happen on a bird while traveling there is no chance of drawing and getting off a shot before the bird takes off.

When you locate a turkey and are ready to call, your set-up is more critical in many ways than when carrying a gun. You must set-up so you

A pocket for the bow tip is also a handy way to keep things steady. Be careful when using a compound bow such as this to make sure the pocket can accommodate the pulley.

can draw and shoot your bow effectively, yet remain concealed. Obviously this can not be done from a prone, semi-prone or normal sitting position which may work well with a gun. Sometimes you can use a downhill sit, one where your legs drop away enough from your seat so you can draw your bow. You should practice in this position and determine your effective field of fire so you know the direction to face when the time comes.

This hunter is set up behind a portable blind. Even so, camo gloves would improve his concealment.

You may also sit on a portable stool or some object. You might even stand if the cover so permitted, however, turkeys seem to pick out a man quickest when he is erect.

My favorite position is kneeling with most of my weight on my daypack or a log under my butt, in other words straddling a relatively low, comfortable object. In this position I have the greatest flexibility in field of fire short of standing. I wear knee pads, the kind found in hardware stores made for people who have to work on their knees. These knee pads can be sprayed with camo paint and are comfortable to walk in if properly fastened.

The reason for the knee pads is comfort. Aside from being in a position you can shoot from and being hidden (more on this in a moment) you must be comfortable. For the same reason as using a cushion under your fanny when sitting you must make yourself comfortable whenever working a turkey. This is important not because you are soft and old but because it is imperative that you be still and not move.

The hiding place is different than with a shotgun for two reasons: First, it must hide you in a more erect position; secondly, it must allow your equipment to blend in with the surroundings. A bow held in the ready

Decoys are popular and effective. But make sure they're legal where you hunt, and pay close attention to the advice in the text on positioning the decoy.

position is harder to hide than a shotgun on your lap no matter how well you camouflage it. Some leave the quiver attached at this time but for reasons previously stated in the chapter on equipment, I feel it is far better to remove it and set it on the ground—handy but hidden.

The type of spot you choose to set-up in should have a more complicated or broken outline than a single tree trunk etc. A thick bush, a fallen tree top or the roots of a fallen tree, are the types of places you should look for. If there are lots of lines and shapes in the background a few more will just blend in.

Sacrifice concealment for a good shooting position. With Western birds unless you look like a pickup truck you are apt to be ignored. Also, when hunting these "less wary" turkeys it is wise to have your arrows where you can reach them with a minimum of movement should you get a chance at a second shot.

One spring in the Black Hills I stood between the trunk of a large ponderosa and a thick juniper, expecting the turkey I was calling to arrive through a break in the top of the rimrock where I had a good open shooting lane. The other open lane was at my back. This turkey, like most, did not come where I expected.

He topped the rimrock about 50 yards on the other side of the juniper, and "homed" in on me from that direction. The ponderosa was now at my back as I peeked through the thick branches of the juniper. I had open shooting on either side of the juniper and I figured it was just a matter of time before the bird headed one way or the other, but he didn't. He decided that the hen must be in the juniper. On he came, a couple of steps one way—"tik, whoom," a couple the other, "tik, whoom," until he was less than 10 feet from me on the other side of the juniper.

At that point I thought I saw an opening to him through the lower branches. I was holding my compound at full-draw, waiting for a clear shot, and could hold it no longer. At the shot the arrow bounced off an unnoticed branch. The startled, but untouched turkey jumped up on a log and looked around. Then as if nothing had happened, he went back into his strut. I slowly nocked another arrow and, in my excitement, missed again. This time the gobbler showed a little more concern as he slowly moved off, but once I was able to cluck at him he resumed his strut.

Now he was about 40 yards away. My desperation shot also missed. As he circled toward the edge of the rimrock, I blew the chance of a 20 yard fourth shot by waiting just a bit too long before he disappeared. Do you think that could happen with an Eastern turkey?

As I said before, the bow should be well camouflaged. The Outline Breaker is a small wire clip that when attached to the bow allows a branch of the bush or adjacent trees to be quickly mounted in front, effectively hiding both bow and hunter. The sight and arrow rest should remain free and clear, however. When you are peeking at the turkey through such a branch you will find it gives you additional confidence.

The next problem to be overcome is holding the bow ready for the shot comfortably and still. To do this effectively the bottom tip of the bow must support the bow's weight. This can be done in two ways. First, obviously, it can be rested on the ground. However, mud, dirt, leaves and debris are not conducive to dependable wheel or cam operation in the case of the compound. The long bow and recurve do not have this problem. It is a good idea to carry a handkerchief sized piece of canvas or heavy weight camo material to place on the ground in order to protect the works at the end of your compound bow—and it will also offer some protection to a long or recurved bow.

If you use a more erect position it is handy to have a bow tip pocket sewed just above the knee in your pants. This pocket should be open at the bottom enough so it doesn't load with debris as you walk through the brush. The bottom opening should be small so the wheel or cam does not go through it and get stuck when you go to pull it out. And it is a good idea to have the top opening wide enough so it is easy to place the bow in it in the first place. You will find this pocket or modified loop handy when bow hunting all other animals as well. With the weight of the bow in the pocket or on the ground cloth it is easy to hold still with arrow nocked and ready to draw.

Our next problem is how to draw the bow when the turkey arrives in range without being seen. We can be clever and lucky by picking a place where the gobbler steps behind a tree at the right moment. We can set-up just over the top of a small knoll and hear him walking before he arrives in view and in range at the same time. We can be even luckier as he struts and turns in front of us his great fan hiding his head for a moment. But good luck doesn't happen often enough and we can get some help from a couple of gadgets.

The most obvious one is a blind, portable, semi-portable or permanent. There are places in all kinds of turkey country where permanent blinds can, and do work. However, this requires a lot of preseason preparation and is not what I call, "in the spirit of the sport."

If you are going to the trouble of using a bow rather than a gun, then why dilute the challenge by a sometimes questionable practice?

A semi-portable blind set up on the occasion of observing a bird in a given spot on one day and then hunting from it on another, is certainly a reasonable and sometimes effective method. The totally portable blind carried by the hunter and used at the set-up of choice can be extremely effective in hiding a hunter's movements. However, it is often cumbersome when carrying it along with your other equipment. Unless used in relatively flat, easily traversed cover, it can slow you down and be more trouble than it is worth. But there are some very successful turkey bow hunters using these blinds, Leroy Baungartz, for one, has had a great deal of luck with a temporary tent blind.

For myself, a better choice, *where legal,* is the use of a turkey decoy. One of the newer ones is inflatable and can be carried folded in your pocket. Others are available in various prices, shapes, in either silhouette or full bodied, and authenticity of finishes.

As the use of decoys increases, and turkeys are exposed to them more often, turkeys may learn to recognize them. The ultimate decoy will probably be a full mounted bird similar to those now used for Canada geese on parts the Eastern Shore.

A decoy properly used distracts the turkey from the hunter and allows you to lead the gobbler to a predetermined spot.

Distracting the gobbler's attention allows the archer a minimum amount of movement. If the old gobbler is really excited, a lot of crazy things can take place without alarming him. The most important thing to remember however is to make sure you cease to call as soon as he spots the decoy. This is very important because unless you are perfectly aligned he will note that the sound is coming from another place. This will draw his attention to you and ultimately confuse or spook him.

Where you put the decoy is very important. First of all, it should be put where it can best be seen. Secondly, it should be where the gobbler can get to it without going somewhere he doesn't want to go, like across a brook or ravine or through some thick brush. Thirdly, it should be put within range, ideally about 20 yards. Fourth, it should be in a shooting lane where any twig or branch etc., between you and the decoy that could deflect an arrow has been removed. Use your pruning shears for this. The placement should also allow the hunter to remain well concealed from all other angles. Finally, if possible, place it near a large tree or some object on one side or the other that the approaching gobbler might step behind while strutting around and circling his new acquaintance. For safety reasons it is also a good idea to have the decoy either facing you or directly away in case an unknowledgeable hunter spots it and fires at it. Decoys are most easily observed when broadside.

At this point I would also recommend a decoy that is full bodied rather than silhouette in shape.

While bowhunting one spring we were set-up in a hedgerow bordering a field at the base of a wooded knoll. A silhouette decoy was in front of us facing away. After calling the gobbler he arrived at the top of the field under the knoll, apparently saw the decoy, strutted and advanced down a fence and wall at the far side until he was opposite us and facing the decoy at which time the decoy simply disappeared to him. He then walked back toward the knoll and after a few clucks to turn him, once again saw the decoy. He went into his strut and started back along the wall only to lose her again. It was a comical situation, but we failed to get a shot at this turkey. Imagine his confusion if he actually came to the decoy and circled it. (Perhaps the answer to the silhouette problem is the use of two or more decoys facing in different directions.)

If all is done right and you now have the gobbler within range, make sure you are absolutely still until his head is hidden behind a tree or facing away behind his erected tail fan. Then carefully bring your bow to full draw, as quietly as possible. All surfaces that your arrow touches should have been made noiseless.

Hold until you have a clear shot at either the high center of the upper body, head on or dead away, or at his wing butt when broadside. At the shot, if you hit, get to the bird as quickly as possible and immobilize him by stepping on his head.

If in the meantime, he is hit and escaping, don't try taking another shot unless he is close and not very mobile. If you are nimble, run to keep him in sight if possible. Otherwise, stand still and concentrate on where he is headed. If he takes off flying, listen carefully for him falling to the ground or through the trees. If he is running, listen for any flapping. If you are running you may not hear these sounds. Arrow hit birds, turkeys included, often fly or run off and then drop dead. Your best chance of recovery (make every effort to do this) is to pay strict attention to where the cripple is going. Remain still for a while and listen. Then hasten to the area the bird went and if he cannot be seen, look in every crack and corner he may have crawled into. Remember, he seldom leaves a blood trail. Except for the feathers severed when he was hit, you probably will not find more until you locate the place where he falls. You might want to try a string tracker or turkey tracker as mentioned in the earlier chapter on equipment.

There are plenty of things that can go wrong with a turkey hunt no matter how well you plan and prepare.

One spring I got a call from outdoor writer and bowhunter, Norm Jolliffe, inviting me to join him and a friend, Ray Olson, on a bowhunt for an old gobbler that gave them the slip for a week.

Before daylight, we approached the ridge where the gobbler was roosting and were gratified to hear him gobble. The plan was to cover a small clearing he usually either flew directly down to or at which he arrived shortly after flying down with his hens.

We positioned a decoy in the middle and each of us set-up in a spot covering all avenues of approach. We in turn noted where the others were so there would be no danger in arrowing one another.

I was given the job of calling. But, because of my care in preparing my set-up under an apple tree, I was late in making my first cluck and the old gobbler had already flown off his roost into the woods above us. However, I soon had him answering my calls which I made on my 1-Hander slate strapped to my thigh.

As he got closer, I had trouble controlling my excitement. He was not coming to the clearing; he was coming down through the woods on my side. I quickly eased around my apple tree and knelt facing the direction he was approaching from. Soon I saw that big black ball of feathers of a strutting tom across a very small creek and up on the top of a bank.

As I continued to cluck and purr to him, he slipped down the bank and set up his strut on a cow path on the other side of the creek. He was only about 25 yards away but overhanging branches of the apple tree prevented a clear shot. As he strutted on the cow path he would come into the open in a position about 35 yards away and at that distance I didn't dare to shoot.

I hoped I could eventually get him closer to me or the others. Norm was in a position where he felt out of it so he started recording the session on tape and got ready to take pictures. All of us could hear the gobbler's distinctive drumming.

For one solid hour he paced the cow path, strutting, and drumming in full view, but partially obscured when within range. "Jacob, if you only had your shotgun he wouldn't be able to do this to you," I thought as I shook all over. Finally he was hidden for a moment and I decided to take the opportunity of trying a different call to see if I could get him to break his pattern.

I carefully rested my bow against the tree, picked up my box call and put a diaphragm in my mouth. I made a short choppy series of yelps on my box and he responded with a double gobble and came running back.

"Aha," I thought, this is what he wants. But I was unable to do it again with the box without being seen so I copied it with my mouth call. With that he dropped his head and sneaked quickly up the bank and out of sight. I tried the box and slate again with no response.

After determining it was all over, I met with Norm and Ray in the center of the clearing. "Did you see him vanish when I used the mouth call?" I asked.

They both nodded and commented that maybe their failures all week were because of this. They had been using their mouth calls as that was all they owned—I rectified this for them before the day was over. The old gobbler had at some time during that week associated mouth call sounds with man and the subtle difference between that sound and yelps made on other instruments was all it took to change the game.

Chapter 15

PHOTOGRAPHING AND RECORDING TURKEYS

A wonderful way to spend time afield and learn more about wild turkeys is to capture them on film or record their sounds on tape. This can be done before or after the hunting season and in some cases during it. No license is needed and no regulations govern it. In all states, except Oklahoma, no electronic calling devices are allowed during hunting season. This means that if you are in the woods during hunting season with a cassette recorder, capable of playing turkey talk, you may get into trouble.

Photographing wild turkeys can be as great a challenge as hunting them, and in some ways a greater challenge. When you are about to pull the trigger or release an arrow you don't worry whether your subject is well lighted or even back lighted, or if the composition is right. Good pictures of wild turkeys are hard to get. We must know a few additional things beyond our hunting skills to get the job done right.

Planning is critical. And special equipment, that we can either make or buy, can be helpful. We don't have to own the best equipment to get good turkey photographs, but it does help sometimes.

I have taken good pictures of turkeys with a normal (50 to 55mm) lens and even with a Minox pocket camera with a semi-wide angle (35mm) lens. Jim Chadwick, Rhode Island's game biologist, has a picture I gave him taken with a simple 35mm camera with a 60mm lens and a regular view finder. The picture is of a couple of strutting gobblers with a group of hens that were later trapped by the state of Vermont and given to Rhode Island for the seed nucleus of their wild turkey population. The story of how I got the picture will demonstrate some hows and how nots in wild turkey photography and is an example of what I call chance photography.

I was on my way to work early one morning when I spotted a group of turkeys feeding in a corn field. Being familiar with the area, I knew the route they would take when they returned to the woods. Having a simple 35mm camera with me, my Nikon single-lens-reflex was home—I never travel without a camera—and not being in a rush, I decided to have some fun. I turned the car around and parked in a spot out of sight where I could follow a brook up to the edge of the woods above the turkeys. I figured the turkeys would follow a stone wall leading up the hill so I approached the area from the other side of the wall. I wanted to catch them out in the open before they got to the woods.

I had ASA 64 Kodachrome film in the camera as it's one of my favorites for chance photographs. If you have any thoughts of selling your photographs for publication or for use in a slide-show presentation you are almost committed to using either ASA 25 or ASA 64 Kodachrome film. These are relatively slow speed films and will compound your problems when shooting in low light, especially when using telephoto lenses.

My final approach was on my belly so as not to be seen over the wall. I anticipated setting up at the wall and perhaps shooting over it at a low spot while thus concealed. But as turkeys often do, they got there before me. I flattened out next to a rock pile about 30 yards short of the wall.

Without a telephoto lens I couldn't do any good unless I could call them over the wall and closer to me. Using a mouth yelper and a prototype 1-Hander, I soon had the hens leading the gobblers over the wall and posing in front of me. It looked great in the viewfinder, strutting gobblers with heads as white as tennis balls, a bevy of feeding hens, an old stone wall as a backdrop and in the distance a view up the valley.

But that was the problem. I was used to a SLR (single-lens-reflex) camera where the viewfinder told me what the lens was seeing. Instead, because of my prone position in the rockpile, my viewing lens, which was above my photographing lens, was seeing turkeys while my photographing lens was seeing rocks and tops of heads. I was lucky enough, however, in 36 exposures to get half a dozen good ones of the turkeys. The rock pictures went into the waste basket.

Another example of chance photography came after I observed some

Bart Jacob uses a "bionic ear" to record turkey talk. Be sure you know your state's law regarding electronic devices. It might be difficult to convince a conservation officer that you're only out there for the sake of research.

strutting birds at the edge of a field and again grabbing equipment in hand crawled as close as I dared along a fence line.

Still about 60-70 yards away, I eased myself up into a multi-trunked fenceline maple. I managed to get partially inside it, where I could shoot through a crotch about head high.

I tried calling but failed to stir the old gobblers. I did manage to pull over some hens and two or three jakes (early spring). They wandered around the foot of the maple clump I was in, trying to make out the turkey in the tree talking to them. I kept up a steady chatter, to hide the camera sounds, as I shot. By cackling, I could get some very grown up poses, both strutting and gobbling, from the young jakes whose beards, only about two inches long, stuck straight out of their chests. With just a simple camera and grabbing an opportunity, I got some good shots.

More often good turkey pictures are gotten through planned photography. Planned photography means using the best equipment at your disposal at a predetermined site or sites to take your pictures because you intended to get them in the first place. It is said that amateurs take pictures while professionals create photographs. Amateurs are said to take advantage of photographic situations when they come across them, professionals are said to first think of the photograph they want to take and then to set up the right conditions for taking that photograph.

Though cameras with fixed lenses and separate viewing lens are okay for chance photography and for taking the occasional photograph of a hunter and his trophy, serious photographers would do well to consider using a 35mm SLR with interchangeable lenses.

Some photographers have good luck using a decoy (as discussed in the previous chapter) to get their subject to a predetermined spot. Photographs have been printed which show amorous gobblers trying to mate with decoys. The decoy, unless you want a photograph of an embarrassed gobbler of course, need not be included in the picture.

Another very valuable piece of equipment used in planned photography is the blind. Baited permanent blinds where legal "out of season" have provided some top-notch pictures. Portable blinds are more practical and there are several types on the market. Given time to construct, I prefer a blind made on the spot with the natural material available there, possibly made more effective with a piece of camouflage material.

Because of earlier recording sessions, a subject for later in this chapter, I

Ben Conger prepares for long-distance photography with a 500mm lens mounted on his 35mm camera. You don't want to lug such gear when hunting, of course, but equipment of this sort is great for spending time in the woods during the off-season or after you've filled your tag.

found a place along a powerline where a big gobbler strutted each morning with his hens. Adjacent to the clearing was a rock outcropping where I was able to build a blind using materials at hand. I set-up in the shade of a rock with the early morning sun at my back.

I set-up before daylight one morning in complete camouflage with a Nikon equipped with auto advance and a 100-to-300mm zoom lens. I was using 400 ASA color film due to the light gathering limitations of the telephoto lens. When the sun came up, I started calling, using loud "where are you" yelps of a hen. Nobody showed ("No shows" is one of the problems with planned photography), but I kept calling. I was about to pack it in when I heard a gobble. A short time later, a large jake cautiously approached within 20 yards and provided me with some excellent pictures. Camera sounds deflated his strut; but continued talk by me including cackles, puffed him back up each time.

In building the blind, I was able to use a sturdy branch on which I could rest the camera while I photographed. This is important for comfort and minimizing movement. Remember, under low light conditions shutter speeds must be slow and a steady camera is important.

The shutter speed should be equal to the reciprocal of the focal length of the lens if the camera is hand-held. For instance: using a 50mm lens the minimum shutter speed for a hand-held camera should be 1/50 of a second. Using a 500mm lens, the minimum shutter speed for a hand-held camera should be 1/500 of a second. With low light conditions such as in the early morning, late afternoon, or even during mid-day when you are in a heavily wooded area, even with the new ultra fast films you will not have enough light to use such high shutter speeds. One solution is to mount your camera on a tripod or brace it on a log, rock or sturdy limb. With your camera braced you can safely use slower shutter speeds, 1/30 of a second with a 50mm lens and 1/250 of a second with a 500mm lens. And if your brace is equal to the support that a good tripod would offer you can cut this in half again—1/15 of a second with a 50mm lens and 1/125 with a 500mm lens.

This striving for a rock-steady camera support, however, proved my undoing once. I located a gobbler on the top of a grassy knoll, a typical strutting area. I got into position early and again was using the Nikon with the 100-to-300mm zoom. This time I hid by a large, fallen oak.

Instead of sitting in front of the oak as I would if shotgun hunting, I got behind it with my legs under a limb and my arms and camera resting on it in a solid comfortable position. Just ahead of me was the open grassy area.

When I found I had enough light by focusing on the grassy area and noting the automatic shutter speed with a given aperture setting, I started calling. The gobbler was anxious, and was in view in moments.

The only problem was, I did too good a job. The gobbler was right at my feet and because of my position, I couldn't get the camera over the branch far enough to get him in the viewfinder. Finally, in frustration, I took some blind shots which didn't turn out very well before he realized something was amiss and took off. If I had only been in front of the oak, I could have had a full frame shot of his snood.

There are many things that can foul-up a turkey photo session. The important things to remember whether doing chance or planned photography, however, are:

First, get as close to your subject as possible. Even the longest telephoto lens requires getting within 20-30 yards, and the longer the telephoto the more light you must have, the steadier the camera must be and the more critical will be focus due to reduced depth of field. A normal lens means getting right on top of your subject, but requires less light, allows a faster shutter speed, and a smaller lens opening (f-stop) which produces greater depth of field.

Second, get as much light as possible. Good light is often hard to get early in the day or in the woods. Wait a little longer for more light if you have to and always try to get your subject to strut in a sunlit spot or out in the open.

Third, make sure the light is striking your subject from the front or side unless you purposely want it back lighted for effect. Some great pictures are made with back lighted subjects against a sunrise or skyline broken by giant oaks. Just plan ahead and get low.

And finally, be aware of composition as this will make the difference between just a picture of a turkey and a great turkey picture. Too often somebody will proudly show you a picture of some black dots out in a field or parts of a turkey, the rest hidden by shadows or brush. You want a picture of a whole turkey, clearly defined and with just enough background to show a viewer that the photograph was taken in a woodland setting but not detailed enough so the viewer tries to identify the trees and ignores the turkey.

Quite some years ago, I did a lot of underwater photography. There weren't too many decent underwater pictures of fish, sharks, etc., at that time and you could sell any that were half way acceptable and recognizable. In time, however, there were enough good underwater photos around that the picture had to be clear, perfectly exposed and state a message to be of interest. Turkey photography took much the same path. For a while any picture with a wild turkey in it was exciting, but now it must be technically good and set a mood to be successful.

If you check the turkey photographs in the leading outdoor magazines you will notice that increasingly the turkey photographs shown are being taken by just a handful of photographers. These photographers are specialists. In some cases they have fenced in several acres of land and have captive flocks of wild turkeys which they can photograph throughout the year in natural settings. They are not waiting for the chance photograph to occur; they are first envisioning the photograph they want and then creating it in a controlled setting.

The same is true in recording turkey talk. A tape that has great lapses in sound or where the calls are barely audible or distorted was once acceptable but is no longer of interest. It is easy, inexpensive, fun, and educational to record turkeys. A good cassette player-recorder, a good hand held microphone and a knapsack is the only equipment necessary other than your calls and your camouflage.

You need not worry about light, you can record at any time during the day and in the darkest woods. The only thing you need to worry about is getting close enough and limiting distortion or extraneous noises. The wind can play havoc on an open mike.

The cassette player should be one that does a reasonable job of recording music, not one of the little pocket models used as a recording memo. It should have a "pause" button which causes less noise when switching it on or off while recording. The small built in microphones are fine for indoor recording but don't have the range for outside. A decent hand held microphone is fine and can be made better with a simple directional reflector I will describe shortly.

If you are really serious about this, there are a couple of good amplifier mikes on the market such as the Bionic Ear used by law enforcement agencies and the Hunter's Ear used by houndsmen to locate their dogs. The amplifier mikes are available with the proper jacks for use with your recorder and can be used with the recorder and a set of ear phones simultaneously so you know exactly what is being recorded. These units are so powerful they have a built in filter that shuts off sounds that are loud enough to damage your ears. This can be a problem however when the sound is shut off to the recorder. When using these mikes, extreme care must be made in adjusting the incoming volume or the tape is just wiped out with sound. If you have an input light or gauge on your recorder, set the mike volume so the light goes on and off and flickers rather than staying on all the time and the gauge works accordingly.

When using these amplifier mikes or any directional mike, set it in a position ahead of you and preferably on the other side of a tree, rock, log or something which isolates you from the recorder so your calling sounds if and when you make them are not overly loud on the final recording.

When I record turkeys, I usually set-up in a place where they can neither see nor get to me. I might set-up under a ledge or on a ledge above them or across a ditch or something they are not likely to come through. I do this for two reasons: one, the turkeys are seldom eventually spooked and two, it usually gives me far more recording time as they spend their time trying to get to me.

I usually start the machine, put it on pause, start my calling and only release the pause button and record when the return calling gets close enough and active enough. Any time the calling slacks off, I push the pause button.

After your recordings are complete, you will find the tapes easier to edit and not all chopped up by using this method.

If I am recording hens rather than gobblers for samples of their yelps, clucks, etc., I do not worry about setting-up where they can't get to me, rather I try to get them in my lap.

I observed a large flock including a couple of gobblers and set-up in a shallow hole under the roots of a blown over tree. I started calling loud and often and soon had the hens headed my way, the gobblers were left behind.

I had my directional mike clamped to a root and facing the oncoming turkeys. When they seemed to lag, I gobbled twice on my Imitator and they headed in my direction. I never made another sound. Various hens, both young and old yelped and I got some wonderful, raspy, anxious yelps from them as they approached.

Then as they got to me the clucking began. I was so well hidden in the hole that the hens milled around me looking for the gobbler, clucking and every once in awhile yelping at some more hens on the way. Their foot steps, and some clucks right into the mike, which startle you to hear, make a fantastic recording. I play it for those who come into my shop and ask how this particular yelp or that particular cluck on their call sounds. When they hear the variety of sounds coming from the real birds, they realize the many sound options they have.

The microphone that made this recording possible was a very inexpensive Radio Shack hand held mike installed in a homemade sound reflector.

From a hardware store I purchased a large diameter clip on reflector light used by photographers, etc. They are made of spun aluminum and once the bulb, socket, and cord are removed, are very light in weight. The bulb, socket, and cord can be saved for use as a drop cord. The aluminum reflector should be scoured with steel wool or a scouring pad to roughen the surface in order to hold paint. I sprayed camouflage paint on the reflector both inside and out. Then I found a large rubber plug such as those sometimes used under the feet of a crated refrigerator. This plug with a hole in the middle was then inserted tightly into the socket hole in the reflector.

The spring clamp was also sprayed with camouflage paint, then re-attached to the rubber plug which had now taken the place of the light socket. The hole in the rubber plug was then enlarged until the handle of the microphone would fit snugly into it after threading the jack and cord through. The head of the mike should be in a position just ahead or about even with the front edge of the reflector.

When used to record, the reflector is clamped on anything handy and faced in the direction I expect the sound to come from. More elaborate parabolic reflector mikes can be made from other materials; however, I found this to be light, handy and adequate. If more sensitivity is desired, the amplifier microphones already discussed are far handier than the big parabolic mikes that can be purchased from specialty shops.

With the right gear and a little luck, you can get some good recordings of some of the rarer sounds turkeys make; good cutts, purrs of all kinds including a good fight sequence, cackles, tree yelps, and even the "wildcat" call of the old gobbler, which I have yet to hear on a tape.

Chapter 16

FALL HUNTING

The fall hunt, where it is allowed, is designed to harvest excess birds in the flock and reduce a given flock to a size that can survive until it breaks up in the spring without undue competition for food.

Fall hunting can also lead to overharvesting in some areas and can be damaging to the overall turkey population if not properly managed. Fall hunting can be a valuable management tool, and there are interesting similarities between spring and fall hunting—such as in the calling of jakes. This is primarily a book on spring hunting, but the picture would not be complete without a section on the fall.

The fall flock of young birds, it has been explained, is very gregarious in nature. The birds have been together since birth and are sometimes joined by other families creating a situation where many birds compete for food in a given range. Sometimes this can be very frustrating to a fall hunter. He may walk miles searching for turkeys without success, but top a rise and run into from 10 to 100 of them.

Successful fall hunters use the turkey's gregarious flocking instinct to harvest birds. If you use your turkey calls properly in the fall, you can experience a situation close to what would occur in a spring hunt as you converse with approaching turkeys. Unfortunately, a smaller percentage of turkeys harvested are taken with a call in the fall than in the spring because many are killed through chance or by hunters who are after other game.

During the spring, you rarely get a shot without calling in the gobbler. However, many fall birds are taken when accidentally flushed by upland bird hunters. For this reason, dogs are allowed in some states during the

Ben Conger checks out a turkey scratching. Look for such areas as evidence of birds in the area, just as you'd check for deer sign before setting up in a particular spot.

fall season. And some hunters have dogs specially trained to find and flush turkey flocks. Fall turkeys are also ambushed at favorite haunts and driven to hunters surrounding a cover. According to hunter surveys, less than 25 percent of successful fall hunters in the Northeast use a call.

The classic method used in the fall is "breaking up the flock" and calling up a dispersed bird. Looking for the flocks or droves, as the westerners call them, of fall turkeys can be a time consuming, exasperating experience or it can be relatively easy.

Basically, it is a matter of a little luck, and knowledge of the area being hunted. If you know turkeys are in the area and food and water are available there, it's usually just a matter of time before you make contact with the flock.

Flocks can be pinpointed if the hunter succeeds in getting into the general area early enough on a calm morning to hear the roost talk just before fly down time, much like gobblers in spring. Roost talk is soft and doesn't last long. However, assembly on the ground may be extremely vocal at times and you have to be "johnny on the spot" to take advantage of it.

It is what happens after contact with the flock is made that we want to talk about here. Many hunters find themselves in this position but do not know the best way to take advantage of it. One of three situations usually develops when the hunter makes contact with the flock.

First, if the hunter suddenly surprises a mixed flock of young birds at close range as when coming over a knoll, over a stone wall or around a ledge, the flock disperses in the classic fashion or "star-burst" with birds flushing in all directions. Usually the hunter is as surprised as the turkeys and fails to get off a telling shot, but his attempts to hit a bird do succeed in helping to thoroughly scatter the flock. This results in the situation we all long for—lots of lost turkeys.

The hunter hides himself at the flush site or in the best place close to the site and waits for the first timorous queries from the lost birds. Early fall, or with seldom hunted birds, calling may begin immediately or we may wait until we hear the first sounds from one of the birds. Generally, the later in the day the flock is flushed the longer we should wait before calling. Sometimes we have to wait 30 minutes to an hour. Often you will first hear some softly repeated clucks or a very soft yelp or two. These should be answered in the same manner.

Soon, you should hear the "kee-kee" or "kee-kee run" which again you should imitate. If done correctly, it won't be long before you have to decide which turkey you are going to try to shoot.

Unfortunately, there can be a snag in this situation. Sometimes the old mother hen gets into the act too soon and begins to call the scattered flock back together. You can't compete with a mother hen. If you can't or don't want to shoot her or if you want to selectively kill a jake, the only thing to do when this happens is to immediately run her off.

The second situation is the other extreme that takes place. The turkeys see the hunter approaching at a distance, but close enough to cause them to flush rather than run off. This usually means all the birds fly off in the same general direction rather than scattering.

When this happens I have had some success with the following method. I move quickly in the general direction the birds flushed until I jump the first bird. Then I go approximately 100 yards more. If I am on a side hill I move up the hill a little to the first good hiding spot. The birds will tend to regroup fast and normally travel up hill away from danger and you should be pretty close to being right among them. Again you should call the same way as with any scattered flock.

The third situation is the most common. It occurs when the bulk of the turkeys flush in one general direction but one, two or more scatter in another or opposite direction. This usually happens when the hunter got off a shot as the turkeys started to run or fly in a flush, thus scaring one or two birds into flight in another direction. This is my favorite situation.

Somehow, the "wrong-way Corrigan" senses it is entirely alone and is a sucker for the first call it hears. Also, in this case you can position yourself to concentrate on the approach of one bird rather than birds from all directions. This is particularly helpful to bow hunters. But be aware, when you start calling one of these birds, be ready! It will often show up at a dead run.

Unless they have been harassed or shot at on the roost, the birds should be found roosting near an area where there is abundant recent sign, which we will talk about in a future paragraph. When you locate a roost you can get good action without breaking up the flock.

There is a certain amount of talk in the roost before fly-down and if you can get into position in the dark without alarming the turkeys, and I have done this successfully many times, you may find yourself surrounded by noisy birds all trying to assemble together after they pitch down.

There will be small groups here and there, jakes usually form their own group, all opening up with their own version of "Hi there" and "come on over." Then there will be the mother hens clucking out their orders trying to get a semblance of organization before moving off to feed. All you have to do is mimic the bird you want, talk hen to hen, jake to jake or even to Mom, and if she doesn't figure things out too quickly you're in business.

Also at a time like this, where legal, it is possible to call more birds in even after one is shot and killed, just keep up the calling after the first bird is down and don't show yourself.

Toward the end of the season, and actually anytime after opening day, there are scattered or lost birds in the woods. For this reason I personally like to hunt fall turkeys by moving through the country side and stopping to make a call every 100 yards or so.

I usually call just before topping a rise so as to reach any birds on the far side or I call down into swales and ravines. When I stop to call, I make sure there is a suitable place to set-up in if I get an answer from a bird just out of sight.

The first call I make is a deep old gobbler cluck. This is a relatively short range call and it will get an answer from a mature gobbler yet, not spook a flock. If I get no answer I make a raspy short series of yelps that can either be mistaken for those of a jake or those of a mother hen.

I have called, received an answer, and then called up lost single mature hens, lost jakes and jakes from a flock with these yelps. You can usually tell when the answer comes from a distance by its urgency, whether it is coming from a lost bird or whether it is just an answer from a flock. If it is from a lost bird, you should set-up right where you are, mimic the other and don't be afraid to keep calling and the lost bird will show up in short order.

If the answer seems just to say "Hey, we're over here," then hurry to get as near as you can without being seen, or ahead of the flock if the answers give you a direction of travel, and try to call a bird out, or call the whole flock in. You may have to move several times giving the impression that you want to get there but don't know how to or can't. Call pleadingly. If you get an answer from a jake, mimic him 'cause these guys seem to like each other's company and are reluctant to walk away from a buddy.

Sometimes in the late fall you will be involved in calling a jake and he answers you with some sharp clucks but won't come. A trick to try at this time is to mix some aggravated purrs in with your answering clucks. You are telling him who is boss and who should do the moving.

This type of fall hunting can be fun. Get into the woods early; listen for roosting or gathering birds, then carefully and quietly slip along a logging road or a bench on the side of the ridge. Enjoy a beautiful fall morning and call before breaking out into a new vista. By the time you start to think you are just wasting your time or you start daydreaming in the early morning sun, you will get an answer and then the tempo of everything including your heart will suddenly change.

Depending on the feed, there may or may not be a lot of scratching to show that turkeys are in the area. Sometimes, when a lot of nuts and seeds are on the ground and until the leaves cover them, the turkeys will simply walk along picking what they want and leave little sign of their passing. I know many hunters who don't understand this and leave the woods for lack of sign.

When turkeys are scratching, learn to identify fresh from old, the direction they are moving, the course they took and the make-up of the flock. When turkeys scratch they usually completely bare the ground, more like a very small deer scrape, because they pick up everything edible in that spot. They feed not just on the nuts and seeds there but also on any bugs, grubs and plant shoots. The leaves are pushed to the rear of the scratching so you know the direction the turkey was going.

The overturned leaves can tell you, upon examination, whether the scratching was done today or yesterday. In an area where you find both, you will know this is where the flock passes through daily.

Look for droppings and from them you can determine the sex and age of the bird. Droppings that look like the letter "J" are from a male, those that look like a curl are from a female. Where both are found it is probably a young flock. Where just larger male droppings are found examine the scratchings. Do they tend to be found at the bases of trees, under the lee of rock outcroppings? If they do, it probably means a small band of mature gobblers have been through.

There are a few fall hunters around that don't fool with the young birds but purposely go after old gobblers. I try this now and again, but my successes are not consistent enough for me to put myself in their league. Dave Harbour, Earl Groves, and others can consistently kill old gobblers in the fall. I have been lucky a couple of times when it counted.

Norm Jolliffe called me from Maine and wanted to do a story on fall hunting particularly with a bow. We got together and got him a story for a bowhunting magazine, then decided to take another day with the shotguns and make another story of it.

I knew a flock was working a particular ridge and we searched for it the next morning with little success. The sign was there and Norm took pictures of me pointing to scratchings, to ash trees full of seed, and various props for the turkey story.

Later we came on some fresh scratchings heading up the ridge. Making a wide loop we neared the top and I was ahead when I stopped to call. I was kee-keeing on a mouth call hoping to sound like a bird some how left behind by the flock.

The second time I called I heard yelps. I turned and motioned to Norm (who was taking pictures of me at the time) to ditch his camera and come running. When he got to me I was just pointing to a place in front of me to set-up in when I saw movement below.

Quickly, I grabbed Norm before he could move forward and sat him down by an old tree root. I lay on the ground behind him and called again, there was no answer but I could now hear the turkeys approaching in the leaves. Young birds don't do that; if you are calling and they are coming, they are also talking. Old birds will occasionally come to a "kee-kee" and I began to believe that was just what was happening.

I switched to my 1-Hander and started clucking. Norm sat with his shotgun resting on a root and never had to move it when five mature gobblers arrived at point blank range. At the shot one flopped down the hill with Norm in pursuit. As he held his first fall turkey up, I had to comment as I took his picture that he should send a copy to his buddy, Ben Lee, explaining that he too shoots nothing but old gobblers in the fall.

It seldom happens like this however, and the man who takes old gobblers regularly in the fall is a very patient, highly skilled hunter. Old gobblers are not as gregarious as they were when young. They do like the company of others like themselves, but probably as much for the added eyes and ears as for companionship.

When two or three old gobblers are scattered, or when a gobbler knows a buddy is roosting in a given area, they can be called in. It may take a long, long time however, because they don't come running in like jakes.

The site of the set-up is important and it usually should be in a high open spot near or above the area where the birds were scattered or roosted. Some calling can be done but it must be done sparingly. The most commonly used call is the single "pop" like cluck of the old gobbler. At times you can use short assembly gobbles or one, two or possibly three old gobbler yelps. I find it difficult to use the yelps because when I make them, just about when they start to sound right, I've got to stop. When a gobbler yelps he knows if he is going to be heard, it happened when he made the first yelp and he seldom needs more.

When two experienced hunters agree to meet at a certain spot in the deer woods, they don't approach the spot yelling and calling to each other. They simply keep their eyes and ears open and wait until they catch sight of or hear the steps of their partner approaching. Old gobblers tend to do the same and as they near the area, they expect to find one another, they

A trophy like this can reward you for preparing well before you go out and plunk yourself down in the woods. The hunter is carrying the bird by its feet, which should only be done to pose for pictures like this one.

seldom call particularly if they have heard the call of another earlier. Rather, they listen for the other walking or scratching and use their keen eyesight.

This means the successful hunter of fall gobblers must conceal himself in the right spot and wait until he believes all the animal witnesses who observed him have now forgotten his presence. Make one or two perfect calls and turn into a statue. In an hour, he might move again just enough to repeat his call. Then several hours later, if he hasn't moved a muscle in spite of numb or cramped limbs, his eyeballs (as they have been casting side to side, like watching a tennis game with your head in a vise) might have finally spotted a movement which turns out to be an old gobbler sneaking in.

As he shivers and shakes, the gobbler slowly approaches. And if his arms aren't too stiff and his fingers too numb at the right time, the hunter might get a shot and become one of those patient men I so admire.

Chapter 17

HUNTING ETHICS AND SAFETY

Turkey hunters are being injured, maimed, and killed by other turkey hunters. It is happening more often than in other types of hunting. No state is free of this problem. First, we have to understand why this is happening and what there is about our sport that is unique and opens up the possibility of an accident.

It's because we hunt turkeys by trying to sound like them. We call to them spring and fall trying our best to imitate them. Not only do we sound like them talking; we also sound like them walking. Or, as some say, they sound like us walking.

Three documented Vermont hunting accidents that relate directly to this come to mind.

The first occurred when a young turkey hunter, sitting in a bush stroking the flip-top lid of a red soft drink can with a stick got a fair semblance of a yelp from it. Another hunter heard the sound, stalked, and located it. He shot at the moving red turkey head in the bush.

One spring two hunting partners split up to hunt turkeys. One shot the other as he sat under a tree calling.

During a fall hunt two young hunters were standing and calling. When they decided to move one of them took only a few steps when a third, unseen hunter shot them in the legs and arms.

Our immediate reaction to these three incidents is that the person who did the shooting was one of those thousands of new inexperienced hunters that our new, fast growing sport is encompassing.

Undoubtedly, newcomers are a problem, but in the three hunting accidents just mentioned, the person who did the shooting was an older, normally responsible, experienced hunter. In all three cases, the person who did the shooting rushed to aid his victim(s). In all three cases, the shooter could not believe what he had done. And in all three cases, the disillusioned hunter announced his retirement from the sport he had enjoyed for most of his life.

We do have a problem with novice hunters and they are the perpetrators of many of our accidents, but we also have a problem with older, experienced hunters who are considered to be responsible and careful in the pursuit of their sport.

What makes a man, who has spent most of his life pursuing game, suddenly become an irresponsible idiot if even only for a moment— "hype" and excitement.

It's a form of buck fever, but different. Those of us who write and lecture about wild turkeys are partly responsible. No football team member is as psyched over his opponent as the turkey hunter is over his. Story after story tells of the struggle and moment of glory involved in killing a turkey. Then out in the woods the story gets re-enacted. The keyed-up hunter hears turkey sounds, sees turkey colors, and in one split second makes a grievous mistake.

There are other factors that compound this problem. Because of the turkey's incredible eyesight and ability to see color we wear camouflage clothing and muted colors when hunting them. This hides us from one another as well as from turkeys.

But camouflage does not make us look like a turkey. And we don't go around shooting things we can't see. The only time a hunter in camouflage should be in danger is when he is invisible to the person shooting at legal game and he happens to be in the way. Camouflage in itself is not dangerous.

Also because a turkey's head can be bright red, white, or blue, we have a situation where some colors that are used to warn us like a red stoplight, innocently used for handkerchiefs or toilet paper, now become dangerous. These colors now might say "turkey." We see a small patch of red when deer hunting and we say "hunter," but see the same when turkey hunting and we might say "turkey."

There are many accounts of turkey hunters being shot while working a call with fluorescent orange gloved hands or wearing a fluorescent orange hat.

Would it help, as some suggest, if instead of full camouflage, we wear all or a minimum amount of red or blaze orange as is required in many states for deer hunting? I doubt it. Without even considering the reaction of the turkey, we are safer when invisible than we are when wearing something which when just a bit of it is in view says "turkey."

I have read of experiments where hunters have successfully taken turkeys while wearing red. Remember, there are all sorts of degrees of wariness among turkeys. How many of you have sat on a deer stand dressed in red with a cardinal on your shoulder or a squirrel on your toe as I have done while dressed in camouflage? These things only happen when you are in complete camouflage. And the actions of small birds and animals in the woods tell the old, hunter-wise gobbler a lot.

What then is the answer? What is the common denominator between careless novice and an overly-excited old timer?

I believe the most important thing is education. Education is not only hunting safety but turkey hunting and its idiosyncrasies. It's how to recognize the sport's potential hazards and when they occur, and how to prevent them.

Teach experienced hunters what to expect. Defensive turkey hunting tricks are as important as the knowledge of when and when not to shoot. As a defensive hunter, make sure your calling position not only hides your entire outline but protects you in every direction from which you cannot see an approaching turkey or hunter.

Don't wear red, white, or blue and remember these colors can show when shirts are open or pants are hiked up while in a sitting position.

Use your calls wisely; don't be tempted to tease an answering hunter. Don't use your gobble unless you fully understand its use. The spring woods are full of shaking box calls, which is how most hunters produce the gobble—I don't know what these guys think they are doing. Although, I remember my first ever attempt at hunting turkeys and I did the same thing.

When you see an approaching hunter, make sure he knows you are a human and not a turkey before you make any motion at all. If you are not set-up on a turkey but are moving through the woods, be aware, you sound like a turkey when you walk and when you call and walk, you can really hype up an anxious hunter.

I have been fooled the other way around a couple of times when I thought I was listening to an approaching hunter, and it turned out to be a turkey. And finally when you are carrying your turkey out of the woods, carry him by the head and perhaps cover him with something that does not look like a turkey.

(Carrying your turkey by the feet should only be done when you want to take photographs. This lets the wings flap and tail spread which makes great pictures. Unfortunately, it can catch the eye of over eager, careless hunters and draw fire. Don't take photographs unless you know you are in a safe area with your bird carried by the feet. Carry your bird by the head and keep it covered if possible.)

An experience I had one spring graphically illustrates a point here. Remember the episode when I left my position to cross an overgrown field and get closer to a gobbler and hen. And, remember, I set-up only to learn he went looking for me while she stayed behind and eventually gave me away when he came back.

Well, several days later I returned for another try. It was a spring morning with a cold, light rain and fog. After listening for a gobble in vain, I set-up against a maple tree just inside the end of the wooded point of land, where the ravine originated, that stuck out into the overgrown pasture and provided the only cover from which one could reach the wooded ridge on the other side.

The gobbler used this cover to explore my initial position on the earlier hunt, and he used it to return to the ravine where he and the hen spent so much time.

I called sparingly and was slowly getting colder and wetter. Having decided there were other places to try and feeling I needed to move to get my circulation going, I made a last series of yelps. From the wooded ridge across the field, I got answering hen yelps.

"Ho ho, she is still with him," I thought, and turned to face that direction. After a while, I ventured a few more yelps. Then through the fog, over a log laying in front of me, I saw a bobbing red and white head. It was heading right for me.

"I'll wait until he comes around the log, one end or the other." I thought. "I only hope his head stays up long enough so I'll know which way he's coming—I've got you now!"

Then out of the fog the bobbing red blob took the shape of a man's head. All of a sudden, I shook all over. I was cold, let down and scared silly.

I whistled as he approached. When he gave signs of hearing I stood up and walked over to him. He was hatless with a red flushed face and white hair. We introduced ourselves and discussed the last few minutes. He said he was partially deaf and neither heard nor made any calls.

I explained that with the bad weather and the appearance of his head he would be better off wearing a hat of some kind and in this case a camouflage one would have been better than a red one. He said he was totally unaware of the hazard potential. If I was over-anxious and fired at the bobbing head, he probably would not have been killed at that range but he could very well have lost an eye.

I am used to taking my turkeys at very close range and for this reason I may have been spared the agony of those hunters who made the mistakes mentioned earlier.

Obviously, we have to think defensively when turkey hunting. Also, we must be absolutely sure of our target. The best way normally to be positive of your target is to make sure it is approaching rather than retreating. Never stalk a turkey; it is unsafe. There are a few instances when very experienced turkey hunters have stalked turkeys with success, but in those cases the turkey was positively identified in advance and the hunter could probably tell you how long the beard was before he started the stalk. When a turkey is coming to you there is plenty of time to identify it and then kill it cleanly when the time is right.

How do we get these points across? We do it every time we write about turkey hunting, every time we talk about it and we take young hunters and new hunters into the woods with us and actually show them how it is done. Calling a turkey in to a friend who is new to the sport, your son or somebody else's can be a terrific experience.

Also, we must make the information part of all hunter safety courses. In almost every state new hunters must take a course before receiving a first license. The addition of turkey hunting safety modules is painless for the instructors. These modules are available from state chapters of the National Wild Turkey Federation and from the National Rifle Association. If we don't include this information in these programs we will soon see separate courses mandatory before a license or permit can be obtained like the courses required in some states for bowhunters and trappers. If we don't do it ourselves somebody else is going to make us do it and we might not like the methods they choose.

This education should also include the ethics of turkey hunting. Ethics by definition are the rules or standards for right conduct or practice. To be unethical does not necessarily mean to be illegal. Therefore ethics are our way, due to our training and thinking, of how we do something. Ethical turkey hunting practices may affect others or only ourselves.

One case is the situation where a hunter takes advantage of another hunter calling turkeys by getting between him and his bird. This is not illegal, but it certainly is not ethical. Neither is it right to move in on another hunter who is already working on a bird. We have to use common-sense here because there are times when we don't know another is working the bird or it may be the bird is obviously not going the other way anyhow. When your behavior involves others, it is usually a matter of putting yourself in their shoes in order to come up with the right answer.

One morning two of us were moving in together on a gobbling jake. We stopped for a moment to pinpoint his location. Hearing something approaching, we turned to spot two more hunters racing toward us. We waved and when they arrived one asked if we were heading for that gobbling bird. When we said yes, he simply wished us good luck and explained where they would continue their hunt so as not to interfere. This made our day as much as did the harvest of the jake a short while later.

There is also a matter of turkey hunting ethics which affects no one but yourself. This relates to what outdoor writers refer to as "the experience of the hunt." The way the hunt is carried out is what counts and not whether you killed a bird. A youngster starting out, or maybe the first time turkey hunter at any age, needs a kill to feel successful. After that, the greatest balm for one's soul is how it was done.

The end does not always justify the means. In most states, it is legal to knock that gobbler out of a roosting tree as long as it doesn't happen before or after legal shooting hours. But where is the satisfaction of harvesting a beautiful bird of trophy proportions this way unless you are starving?

Sometimes, however, peer pressure, or commercial involvement with the sport, drives us to be successful and it becomes extremely important to produce. I know of instances where colleagues reported opening day birds killed in one state that were taken in another a day earlier. Those standing around admiring don't know what happened and you probably will not get arrested for it, but in your own mind, you know. If your turkey hunting is reduced to this, it can no longer be the marvelous experience this whole book has talked about.

Rather than end on that note, however, let me tell you a tale of how "the experience" got the best of me.

I was fall hunting in New York and before dawn, I heard a roosting flock. I set-up under the ledgey spur of a ridge they were on and when they flew down, they went the other way.

After a short climb to the top, I quietly worked my way down the side over which they disappeared. I heard scratching below me and carefully peered around a tree. There was a mature gobbler, magnificent beard bouncing on the ground as he alternately scratched and picked up his breakfast.

"A chance for a mature bird," I thought and quickly backed out of sight. I picked a spot a few feet away to set-up and call from. A loud cluck, then silence, another and some more, finally I made one old gobbler yelp and still nothing happened. After almost an hour, I decided on another look. As I peered around the tree again, I saw the gobbler's scratchings, but no gobbler.

Then I realized, when I first saw him, he was only 25-yards away and an easy shot. But it never occurred to me to shoot. Up 'til then, and since, I have never killed a turkey I did not call in. Letting that ethic overwhelm me at the moment cost me the only chance I had at a mature gobbler that fall. Stupid? Maybe. But somehow it doesn't bother me that much.

Chapter 18

PREPARATION OF TURKEYS

Wild turkey, properly cared for, is never strong or gamey. Properly cooked, it is never dry, and the breast meat of even the oldest gobbler is never tough. The greatest gift you can give a land-owner host is one of his wild turkeys you have harvested, particularly if he is a farmer and his prime hunting time is taken up with chores.

The whitetail hunter may say this is fine but it can't compare with his combination of meat and trophy rack to hang on the wall. To a turkey hunter, the beard and spurs of a gobbler are just as much of a trophy as any set of antlers. What's more, if desirable, the whole bird may be mounted. The trophy, which is not as large as a moose, caribou, or elk head can be placed in a corner of your den under the lights to show off its glorious iridescent colors. Try and get away with a full body mount of one of those others in your house. The wild turkey, in my opinion, is the finest tasting trophy a hunter can harvest.

The best time to start thinking about the preparation of a turkey is when it is lying at your feet. You have decided the great bird is not a figment of your imagination, nor is he about to go anywhere.

He is real; he is dead. You can't help but look at him for a while, then you snap to your senses and look at his beard and his spurs. Tag him now if the law requires it.

If he is the biggest, best gobbler you ever shot and if you anchored him with a good head shot so not too many feathers are misplaced, you may

If you have enough space, a full mount of a flying gobbler makes an impressive trophy-room display.

want to have him mounted. This is the time to decide. If there is any doubt, it is still the time to treat him as if he were to be mounted.

Take the garbage bag you brought for this event from your vest or pack and unfold it. Examine the head of your turkey and if it is bloody, and it probably will be, cut a corner off the bottom of the garbage bag. The hole should be no larger than the neck of the turkey. Place your turkey carefully in the bag pulling the head through the hole, this will prevent blood from getting on the feathers. Then cinch up the bag around the turkey's feet and tie on your carrying strap. The garbage bag will prevent the wings and tail from flopping and will keep the feathers clean and in place.

Leave the bag on the turkey when you place it, undisturbed, in a cooler or in a cool place. Only after it has been cooled down should it be frozen for shipping or for storage until it can be taken to a taxidermist.

If you live in Virginia and you killed your turkey in Texas and want to get him home to your taxidermist, you need to box him so he will stay frozen. In most cases a frozen turkey boxed properly will stay frozen for several days if you are driving and will definitely make the trip home if you are flying.

Experienced hunters get to a bird fast when it falls, and they remain ready to make it stay down if necessary.

Get a sturdy cardboard box large enough to hold your turkey without damaging wings and tail feathers. Line the bottom of the box with several layers of newspapers. Then place your bagged, frozen bird in the box and pack scrunched up newspapers everywhere around the bird. Pack it tight

A knife or pruning shears can be used for the wings. If you don't want the feathers yourself, save them for fly-tying friends.

with as much newspaper as you can and make sure there is no part of the bird not insulated with paper. One hunting buddy of mine uses his dirty laundry from the trip along with the newspapers to fill the box.

Close up the box and tape or tie it tight. Leave the whole thing in the freezer, if you can, until you are ready to leave. If you are flying, check the box in as luggage and tell the attendant it is frozen and it will be so marked and stored in the unheated portion of the baggage compartment. Frozen turkeys for consumption and frozen meat of all kinds can travel effectively this way.

If you are bringing home an elk, pack the meat as above in boxes weighing no more than 70 pounds each and they can go on the plane with you as excess baggage and your charge for such is a fraction of the cost of having the meat air-freighted home.

Anyway, back to the turkeys. Your taxidermist will want the frozen bird intact; do not dress it out.

If, on the other hand, you are not interested in mounting the turkey and you cannot think of letting your taxidermist end up with all that beautiful meat, it is still not necessary to immediately dress out your bird. If you are going to pluck it within a few hours, it is easier not to open up the body cavity as I will explain shortly.

On the other hand, if you plan on taking it home with you tomorrow and it is warm, it will be advisable to clean it. You can do this when you get to a place where you have some plastic bags and paper towels handy and some soap and water for your hands. I know hunters who insist on cleaning out crop and body cavity in the woods, but unless you have a lot of time to kill this is unnecessary and you will end up with blood all over yourself and your car.

If your bird is of trophy size and you want to enter him in the record books, weigh him with proper scales, measure his beard and spurs and enter all this information on your application in front of the proper witnesses. A good place to do this is at the check station in those states that use them. Next, finish your picture taking because this will be the last time your prize will be fully dressed and presentable.

Plucking your turkey can be a chore or a cinch. If you dry pluck him, it can be a chore, but not nearly as bad as plucking a goose. My recommendation is to scald your turkey first and if you do this you will never pluck one dry again I promise you.

I have a friend out west who once commented that he really didn't enjoy shooting turkeys anymore because of the chore of plucking one. I showed him how to scald and he got such a kick over the ease of plucking that he was helping everyone else with their turkeys. It was almost as if he was getting revenge on those earlier birds.

The first step is to cut off the beard, take a little flesh with it. Rub Borax into the flesh and leave in a place away from dogs, cats, and mice to dry.

Scalding the bird first will make plucking much easier.

The next step is to cut off the tail. This is done by first removing the feathers underneath it to expose the pope's nose. Cut through this from the under side but be careful not to go through the skin on the top side. Skin back the top side for about one inch and then cut the skin off. This will leave a nice fan of iridescent rump feathers on the tail. Put the tail aside for the moment.

The first step in processing is to cut off the tail of the bird. It's an easy chore with a sharp knife.

Next you must remove the wings. Pull out the wing and notice the web of skin that encloses the second joint. Cut through skin and joint and remove each wing. Don't throw them in the garbage because if you don't want them, your fly-tying buddies will.

Now cut off the feet at the top of the tarsus on the naked part of the leg. Save these.

While you have been whacking up your turkey, your scalding pot should have been heating on the stove. Some use a metal scrap basket or small garbage can for this, but if you can get your hands on one of those old fashioned boilers that straddle two burners, it's perfect for the job. Put enough water in the pot to cover at least half of the bird when immersed. Bring the water almost to a boil, when those little bubbles start coming off the bottom, it's about right.

Take your pot outside and grasping the turkey by the head immerse him in the hot water. Use a stick to hold him under and leave him there for 15 to 20 seconds, then turn him over and do the same. Make sure you get all of him, particularly the back and the wing butts where feathers seem to hold tightest.

Remove and drain him, then grab a hand full of feathers. If they come right out, you are all set to continue, if not immerse him again. Do not overdo it for if you cook the skin, it will tear easily. What you are trying to do is soften the fatty tissue that holds the feather in its follicle.

Hang the bird up by the head over a garbage can and go to it. Not only should the feathers come off in handfulls, but also the pin feathers should come clean and the bird will start looking like a "butter-ball."

When you have finished with the plucking, it is time to clean your bird. Open up the chest and remove the crop, usually it can be removed intact. It can be examined for food contents. (In the fall it will indicate what the bird was feeding on.) The fatty breast sponge is removed by some at this time, it might look better removed, but it is not necessary to do so. Then the exposed windpipe should be cut. Next carefully cut around the vent and continue your cut up to the base of the breast bone. If you did it right, the intestines can be pulled free from the bird.

Now you have to get your hand dirty so have a bunch of paper towels ready. Also have a small plastic bag handy. Put your hand in the body cavity, it is a tight squeeze, and grab. What you come out with is the gizzard. Cut around the gizzard so you can open it like a clam and skin out the inside. Remove the connecting intestine, wipe off the gizzard and place it in the plastic bag. Next go back inside and bring out the heart and liver. Trim and wash off excess blood, wipe and place in the bag. Now go back inside and grab anything that will come including windpipe and lung material. When you are satisfied you have everything, wipe out the cavity well with your paper towels. Cut the head off at the neck and he should look like he came from the market place.

If you are going to eat him immediately make sure you have wiped off all blood and put him in the refrigerator along with your bag of giblets. If you are going to freeze him, wrap him with freezer paper, store the giblets in his body cavity, mark the package, including the date, and put it in the freezer.

In the South, fried turkey is popular. It can be very good for a change, but I think it either originates from getting out of plucking the bird or from past times when it was common to harvest a bird for camp meat.

In this case enough feathers are pulled from the breast so as to make an incision with a knife, through the skin, top to bottom of the breast bone. Then pull back the skin on either side to expose the entire breast. The breast meat is then sliced off the bone in two large fillets.

The legs are then exposed, cut off at the thigh joint, and skinned. The drum stick is then cut off and saved for soup. The thigh is boned out. The two boneless thighs and two breasts are then cooled off in a refrigerator. A recipe for fried turkey can be found at the end of this chapter.

Let us now go back to the things we have set aside: beard, tail, wings and feet. The beard needs little further care. After the flesh has dried and hardened, it can be trimmed. If the beard is crooked, you can straighten it by placing it in a folded piece of cardboard and holding it there with several rubber bands. In a few days, it will stay in the position you placed it. The beard can now be displayed by itself or in a tail mount or it can be inserted and glued into a shot shell. (To make a shotshell beard mount, punch out the primer of the shotshell and insert a rawhide loop through the hole. Knot the rawhide to keep it from pulling back through the hole and draw it up tight. Then insert and glue the beard. Shotshell beard mounts of this type are usually worn around the neck like a string necktie.)

The tail needs some more work. Remove the meaty portion, not the yellow fatty tissue that holds the feathers. Also cut out the small piece of tailbone that you can feel leaving just the feather bases and the yellow fatty material. A little meat won't hurt.

Rub Borax on all the flesh and skin and nail the tail to a board in the fanned out position. Use as many nails as are necessary to get a nice even

This turkey fan is a bit ruffled here and there, but it will make a nice wall mount. It's being stretched prior to mounting. At the base of the fan, you might want to display a picture of the hunt or the shell casing and a name plate showing the place and date of the kill.

job because once it dries, this will be its final shape. Sprinkle a little more Borax on the fleshy parts and if you want to hasten the drying use a little salt mixed in to help pull out the moisture. Make sure the rump skin and feathers are properly arranged. Again place the tail to dry where dogs, cats and mice cannot spoil it.

When thoroughly dried brush off the Borax. Remove any excess dry hardened flesh and spray the entire tail with household bug spray. Spray enough on the fleshy portion to leave a residue and let it dry. Taxidermists use arsenic for this purpose, but the main thing is to prevent any future damage from insects.

Any broken feathers can be glued. Sometimes a toothpick is inserted into the two parts of a broken feather to restore its shape. If a feather has fallen out and the follicle is intact, the feather can be replaced by wetting the follicle and inserting a Phillips head screwdriver of the same diameter,

Here's a finished wall mount that incorporates the gobbler's beard and an information plate.

working the water into the follicle and then insert the feather. It will stay when it dries.

Bent feathers can be carefully steamed and they will take their former shape. Now you can mount your tail anyway you desire.

A leather wall mount kit is available for hanging your tail and beard and it includes a brass plate for engraving such things as who, where, when and how big. Turkey tail feathers alone can be worked into a beautiful Christmas wreath, a dried flower arrangement, or other form of decoration. Remember the American Indian prized them over any other for his adornments.

Turkey wings can be fleshed out and dried like a turkey tail, but more often the feathers are removed. This is easiest to do if you soak the wing butts in the scalding pot after you have removed your turkey. If you don't do that you may literally have to cut your feathers out of the wing—they are held in that tight. Wing feathers may be made into decorations, bobbers for fishing, old fashioned quill pens and into flies for fishing.

If you have killed a fall hen, save the wing bones and make a wing bone call or send them to somebody who will do it for you. Gobbler wing bones also make good yelpers, but are more difficult to manage properly.

The feet can be dried, nailed in the position you would like them. A little Borax rubbed over the cut joint is all you need. Most hunters prize just the spur. Dwain Bland and Rob Keck have made good looking spur necklaces. Instead of bear claws or shark teeth, the spurs are threaded on a thong with maybe a bead or two between them. Dwain's necklace is made up of large spurs from all subspecies that he has killed.

To prepare the spur for a necklace, cut the leg off just above and below the spur. Skin this portion baring the bone. Remove the marrow and tendon and clean. If the bone is to be left exposed you can bleach it with a strong Chlorox solution, but don't get any on the spur. Dwain has had a jeweler cover the leg bone with silver. The spur is then added to the necklace by threading the thong through the hollow bone. You may simply want to add your spurs to the lanyards on some of your turkey calls.

Another thing that might be mentioned that is used are the iridescent breast feathers. Ladies' neck pieces have been made using these and hat bands. One thing is certain there is plenty of trophy in that old warty-headed gobbler.

Now for the good eating part. If I am going to roast my turkey instead of stuffing it with a conventional stuffing, I stuff mine with cut up apples,

Bart Jacob admires the tailfeathers of a wall mount. Note the mount of a jake with its elongated center feathers.

wild apples, if possible. This adds moisture to the bird rather than drawing moisture from it.

Using the giblets, I make my stuffing separate, or make giblet gravy. Then I put the apple-stuffed bird in a roasting pan with bacon on the breast or rub it with butter or margarine, and cover with a tent made of foil. This keeps the bird self basted as it cooks, and even steams it a bit which helps an old bird stay moist and tender. I roast the turkey in a

Bart Jacob shows his pleasure as he checks a mounted gobbler.

350-degree oven for 20 minutes per pound, turn oven down if it looks like the turkey is getting too brown. Then, if necessary I remove the foil tent for the last 45 minutes to an hour to brown the breast. It is then ready to serve.

There are other recipes for roasting turkeys to be found in outdoor magazines and books on game cookery. If your turkey is small, you may wish to have it smoked. Because a wild turkey is built differently than a domestic one, it will not have as much meat on it, however the meat it has is far superior. A small smoked turkey sliced for hors d'oeuvres will be a hit in any crowd.

A turkey may be brined in an ordinary ham brine, or it can be treated with a special poultry brine. You cannot over-brine a turkey and you can spoil it by not brining it enough. If you are not experienced in this, get good advice or let a professional do it. The cured turkey is then placed in a smoker and should remain there for the proper amount of time. I smoke a 10 pound turkey about eight hours. Too much smoking and too much heat will dry out your turkey.

We mentioned fried turkey and this is a smart way to have wild turkey in camp. Take the boned thighs and breasts from the refrigerator which has cooled the meat for easier slicing. Cut the meat across the grain into slices about one quarter of an inch thick. Dip the slices in flour or a batter of milk and egg and roll in bread crumbs. Fry the slices in a fairly hot pan for just a few minutes per side. Remove and keep warm until ready to serve with or without gravy.

And one of my favorites. After we have cleaned up all the breast meat and the tenderest part of our roast turkey, we have the makings of a great wild turkey soup. Cut up the carcass with game scissors into pieces that will fit a big pot and add the legs. Add chopped onion, celery and carrots. Cover with water. Bring to a boil, cover and reduce to a simmer. Simmer until meat falls off the bones. Remove the meat from the bones in chunks, return to broth, salt and pepper to taste and add chicken bouillon if necessary. Add rice or noodles and cook until tender. We often freeze it to enjoy on a cold winter's day.

The wild turkey is such a flavor treat that nothing should be wasted.

Chapter 19

ORGANIZATIONS AND THE FUTURE

The responsibility for the future of this magnificent bird rests with you and me, with our local hunting clubs and organizations, with state wildlife agencies and the federal Department of Interior, with farmers and small land owners, with ranchers and large timber companies, and with those who oversee state and national parks, forests, and wildlife areas.

But who will coordinate these efforts so that an individual, group, or organization doesn't work against its own best interests?

That's where an organization like the National Wild Turkey Federation comes in. Founded in 1973, it is dedicated to the wise conservation and management of the American Wild Turkey. Tom Rogers was its founder and in the early years it was patterned after the well-known, and successful, Ducks Unlimited. State and local chapters were formed to raise funds for proper use by the parent organization.

One thing, however, was very different. Turkeys, unlike ducks do not migrate. They do not nest in one area, perhaps allowing management for higher production, and then provide sport throughout the country. Turkeys are local birds needing local management and each locality has its own set of problems.

Local problems vary greatly—strip-mining and the release of game farm birds in Pennsylvania; extensive clear-cutting of large acreages in parts of the South, and deer hunters who blame the turkey for the decreasing deer herd in Vermont are a few examples. Each problem may be unique in its own locality or it may be widespread. The state and local chapters therefore became involved actively and financially on the local level and felt this was where their efforts should be funneled. Local chapters had many members that were not members of the national organization.

There was a period of change for the Federation out of which came today's makeup and philosophy. Now all members of state and local chapters are members of the parent organization. No dues are paid locally, but the state chapters receive a rebate on each national membership.

The national organization has moved to new headquarters which, through donations by the membership, special drives and substantial contributions, provides the facility from which coordination of research and management can take place.

The Wild Turkey Building in Edgefield, South Carolina, where the national organization is now based, also houses a computer. This will aid in achieving these goals and in the efficient administration of the organization. It will handle the World Gobbler Records so aptly started by Dave Harbour, a service of great interest to hunters as well as to researchers.

The National Wild Turkey Federation is providing grants for local research; support for trap and transfer projects; rewards for those who provide information leading to the arrest and conviction of poachers; scholarships for deserving persons; an effective youth program; and sponsorship of Wild Turkey Symposiums. These bring together hunters, turkey biologists, land owners, and industry. The Federation will continue to grow as long as the people who care about wild turkeys support it and provide talented input into its programs and projects.

For obvious reasons, the National Wild Turkey Federation cannot support commercial interests. If it did, it might be accused of sponsoring this outfitter or that, or this manufacturer or that. For this reason, there will probably be other organizations, perhaps an association of turkey call manufacturers. One such new organization is the American Turkey Hunters Association headquartered in Mansfield, Pennsylvania. This organization was formerly called the Professional Turkey Calling Association and was founded by Bob Clark and Ben Rogers Lee.

The association coordinates the interests of hunters, contest callers, and calling equipment manufacturers. It also has a youth program and a hunter-host exchange program. It is through this organization that the All-American Turkey Calling Championship, a professional calling contest with substantial financial rewards is held.

Organizations such as these, through their magazines and newsletters, let those who are involved with wild turkeys know what is going on. And through their seminars, meetings and conventions, they receive the input of their membership. This all helps in the coordination of efforts toward the effective management of wild turkeys.

The grants-in-aid program of The National Wild Turkey Federation provides some of the funding for such projects as establishing wild turkeys in marginal ranges and the reestablishment of certain subspecies into historical habitat or the establishment of the same in new, but acceptable habitat.

The efforts of state wildlife agencies, aided by these projects, has led to a situation where wild turkeys are found in many more places outside their historical range. The diverse nature of the habitat requirements of each of the subspecies plus their ability to survive in sometimes marginal range has allowed the use of different subspecies in the creation of new flocks.

We discussed the success of the Merriam's turkey in the Black Hills of South Dakota, but the Black Hills are but a small, environmentally unique part of the state. Most of South Dakota is open flat grassland and here the Rio Grande turkey is being tried. These Rio Grande birds are from Oklahoma where they already carry some Merriam's blood. Texas now has Eastern and Rio Grande birds as does Oklahoma. Oregon has Eastern, Rio Grande and Merriam's, as does Nebraska, and California. California now has some hybrids as does Kansas, Minnesota, and Nebraska. The ranges of the new implants are bound to overlap.

Historically, there was a certain overlap between Merriam's and Rio Grande in the West and these hybrids can be found in northern Texas and Oklahoma. The same thing occurred in the east between the Osceola and the Eastern in northern Florida, southern Georgia, and along the coast to North Carolina. The Eastern bird has been established as far west as California. It had the largest original range and is perhaps the most adaptable of the subspecies. It can survive all the way north to the Canadian border—which it has already crossed in a few places—and is prevalent in the south.

By using the individual characteristics of the various races, the trapping technology that has developed, the ease of air transportation, and the cooperation now existing between states, wild turkeys are being tried in many environments. States are giving away turkeys in a cooperative spirit, or are trading the birds for something they want. Oklahoma trading Rio Grandes to South Dakota for fish (walleye) is a good example of mutually beneficial exchanges.

What does this all mean? First, there are turkeys out there already for people to hunt in places they never were before, and new populations are developing. It means that there will soon be huntable turkeys in all states but Alaska. Also, it means there are more and more hybrids out there and these birds are starting to fill all the gaps between environments typical to a particular subspecies. Biologists are pleased with their efforts, and so are sportsmen.

What happens when we end up with a bunch of hybrids? Do we build a super bird capable of living anywhere or do we weaken the bird's survival capability as sometimes happens when even a fraction of domestic blood is introduced? One thing is apparent—we dilute the pure strains.

But I'm not sure this is the right answer, and the Technical Committee of the National Wild Turkey Federation at the 1983 Convention decided, and I quote from an article by Dr. James Earl Kennamer in *Turkey Call* Magazine: "After much discussion, the technical committee passed a resolution concerning hybridization of wild turkey populations. The essence of the resolution stated that the committee, in accord with state wildlife agencies, wishes to foster and encourage definitive research into the effects and long-range impacts upon the survival, welfare, and management of the wild turkey resulting from planned or inadvertent hybridization of taxonomic subspecies. The committee further resolved to urge a conservative approach toward turkey relocation projects which may lead to hybrid populations, until definite findings concerning the full range of potential ramifications of hybridization can be determined."

To me, this seems a wise approach. Overzealous activity due to the success of modern trap and transfer methods and the availability of the resource may lead to problems similar to those found a generation ago when anxious sportsmen released pen raised birds in areas where wildlife agencies were releasing wild, trapped birds.

In my opinion it seems a shame to dilute the pure strains. Once you have studied and hunted each of the subspecies and learned to admire the individual beauty of each as well as their environmental differences, it would be a crime to eliminate this individuality. I hope that through the efforts of all responsible and through the leadership of the National Wild Turkey Federation and other caring and influential organizations, the introduction of new subspecies within a region where a pure strain has survived historically will not be allowed.

However, new regions where no strain exists should be open for stocking with any suitable strain. I hope my grandson can go to southern Florida and bag an unmistakable Osceola in a Cypress swamp or to south

Texas for a typical Rio Grande or the Colorado mountains for a classical Merriam's hunt or to an oak-covered Vermont ridge for his magnificent Eastern.

This is not to say the current project to reestablish Gould's turkeys in southwestern New Mexico and southern Arizona should not continue, to the contrary it is a most exciting project. The Gould's turkey, only found in good numbers in the Sierra Madre Mountains of Mexico, was native to these regions and small numbers of them do exist there in a protected state today. Presently, it is almost impossible to arrange a spring hunt for these birds in Mexico.

Cooperative arrangements have been made between the states of Arizona and New Mexico, our government, and the government of Mexico to obtain and release a substantial number of Gould's turkeys in the United States and is exciting Mexican wildlife biologists as well as our own. Part of the program, partially financed by a grant-in-aid by the National Wild Turkey Federation, is to train Mexican biologists in the techniques of trap and transfer and provide the citizens of Mexico with some of their own trapped turkeys to be retained for their own use. This should provide two things: 1) it makes the Mexican people more aware of this resource and soon it may be relatively easy to plan a spring hunt for the Gould's turkey in the picturesque Sierra Madres of northwestern Mexico; 2) if the Gould's subspecies can be isolated in parts of Arizona and New Mexico and managed to keep its genetic integrity, i.e., no crossing with resident Merriam's, we may someday have a fifth race of turkeys to hunt in the United States.

Presently, I'm planning to try for a new "Royal Grand Slam." Such is the life of a turkey hunter.

Chapter 20

UPTIGHT TURKEYS

Starting in 1986 and for the next ten years I hunted turkeys exclusively with the bow and was able to take quite a few gobblers including a grand slam with this equipment. The last few years I have done the same, but as yet the grand slam with a 20 gauge blackpowder shotgun of my own make.

When one hunts turkeys with either of the above, one has to get them very close. Therefore "uptight" refers to the proximity rather than the mood of the turkey.

Bow range for me is 20 to 25 yards and black powder range is bow range. Working a gobbler in this close takes a few tricks and great patience, but it also provides a wealth of experiences.

As said earlier, the wild turkey gobbler has keen vision and an extraordinary ability to perceive movement. He reacts to what he sees without hesitation. Added to this is an uncanny sense as to where a sound, such as your calling, is coming from. The closer he gets the more acute these senses become. Therefore if you expect the gobbler to come close, you have to be well hidden and movement must be limited. Secondly, if you have been calling, the gobbler will be completely spooked if there is no apparent source of the call i.e. no hen in sight.

First, the most obvious way to be hidden is through the use of a portable blind. Camouflage blinds (those made by Double Bull Archery are some of the best) can be very effective and don't seem to bother the turkeys. They are very portable and fast to set up and take down. But even these blinds require two people to effectively carry all the gear and employ them unless a blind is placed before the hunt and this often puts limitations on the hunter and his effectiveness.

I prefer making a natural blind where and when the opportunity arises for each given situation. There are ways to do this and most require the use of a good ratchet-type pruning shear. Instead of looking for a big tree or stump to set at your back, look for a thicket or brush pile. I take my shear and cut out a nook that I can get back into with enough cover behind and both sides to hide me, leaving a clear shot out to my decoy. More about decoys later.

In the brush country of Texas most large Mesquite trees will have their bases surrounded by brush and "pencil cactus." These are good places for making your nook but be careful in getting the cactus out of the way as it has a habit of biting. In the same country there will be brush piles where clearing has been done, they make great blinds as long as you first check for snakes. In Mirriam country you will find juniper thickets though somewhat harder to cut out. Osceola country is full of palmetto thickets and the shears will cut the green palmettos. Stay away from the dead fronds as they make too much noise.

The first Osceola I was to arrow happened in the Big Cypress of southern Florida. He was roosted at the edge of a natural clearing. I snuck in before daylight and was having a difficult time finding a potential blind when I spotted a narrow game trail entering the clearing. I set up a few yards back in the trail and cut a few palmettos, which I stuck in the ground at my back. My decoy was in the clearing in front of me. I called once when I heard the gobbler fly down and after almost an hour of gobbling he circled my position. I spotted him through the brush strutting toward my decoy. I pulled my bow just before he stepped into the clear and with the shot he went down. I ran to him, placed my boot on his head and watched as he flapped and struggled. Soon all movement stopped and the feathers of his breast raised then quivered and relaxed. I congratulated myself and stepped up to retrieve my decoy. I turned to see my so-called dead turkey running like heck for the palmetto brush with my arrow in his thigh. I never did recover that bird and if he lived through it I'm sure that I am not the last predator that he has fooled by feigning death.

Secondly, to fool the gobbler's ears, it may be possible to set up in a way that he does not come into sight and therefore can not see the source of the turkey talk until he is within range. Otherwise one must use a decoy. Decoys are now legal almost everywhere. I have used all kinds of decoys but for filming the hunt nothing beats the "stuffer." And one made from a legal Eastern hen, although slightly different in coloration, is accepted by all subspecies. While filming our bowhunts, dominant hens of all kinds have pounded our decoy into the ground. One such Rio Grand hen went into a full strut in front of the decoy. Hens can be just as aggressive as toms. Along with the interaction one would expect from gobblers we

The author and a Rio Grand shot with his 20 ga. under hammer at 17 paces.

have had some amusing encounters with other animals. There have been several coyote attacks, in one after pouncing on the decoy the coyote slinks off out of embarrassment. One morning in Florida, with good friend and video photographer Bob Benson, I had placed my decoy in a field with a push button call tied to its foot and the line to operate it back to the blind. A herd of cattle soon gathered, circling the decoy, their noses almost touching it in curiosity. When I pulled the string and the decoy skwalked there was an immediate stampede. We laughed so hard that we spoiled that hunt.

My "stuffers" are Eastern hens mounted in the usual way except a block of wood has been glued inside the foam form and through this block of wood is a heavy wire that forms an elongated staple. The legs and feet are run through by this staple and pivot at the point of the hips in the wooden block. This allows folding the legs up when transporting and by using a thin wire attached to said legs the decoy can be placed in various degrees of erectness by simply hooking the tag end of this wire into the foam behind the skin of the breasts.

I was hunting Rio Grands with friend and cameraman Jeeper Morrill. A dominant gobbler was carrying on in a field beside us but paying little attention to our calling. A group of non-dominant birds however reacted every time we called and came in for a look-see. Hoping to get the dominant bird I would quit calling until the group got disinterested and left. However as soon as I called again . . . back they came. This went on several times until we decided that we had better make the most of the opportunity at hand. The only problem now was that the gobblers now had gotten sick of the whole thing and would not approach the decoy. I had previously attached a string to the decoy so that I might give it some motion. Finally during our stand off Jeeper whispered "pull the decoy down." As soon as I had done this the group of gobblers rushed in and as one tried to jump on the now prostrate decoy I arrowed it. We now call this trick the "immor-ill" maneuver.

Another advantage of a good decoy is the fact that you can get away with certain amount of movement without spooking the gobbler because if the decoy shows no signs of alarm there is a calming effect on the gobbler. This fact allows one often to have more than one shot. I always have an arrow or two ready for the retrieval with the least amount of motion. It is also possible when a group of gobblers approach the decoy if one or more get skittish and start moving off another of the group sensing an opportunity to get to the decoy without competition will allow you to get a shot.

For bowhunting I have other pieces of equipment that help with the setting up properly. I made a combination seat and decoy carrier by welding a metal frame which forms a half cylinder. Shoulder straps are attached to the flat side and a thick foam rubber cushion is attached to the rounded outside forming a comfortable seat when laid flat side down on the ground. The inside cavity is big enough to hold a double-ended bag, drawstrings at both ends to hold the decoy and allow it to be placed and removed without ruffling the feathers. A folding stool and separate double-ended bag, each with their own carrying strap, is also sometimes used.

I have also rigged my bow so that it is ready for action with the minimum amount of motion. I machined out of bar stock a head that attaches to the end of a front stabilizer. This head contains two inserts into which a pair of legs made from old aluminum arrows can be screwed forming a tripod with the end of the lower bow limb. The bow with the arrow nocked and on the rest can then be placed on the ground at your side ready for action. This seems to have no effect on shooting the bow accurately.

As with any type of hunting the ammunition used and the placement of the shot have a tremendous influence on your success. The arrow itself needs only be one that you are comfortable shooting. The head however and the way it is rigged is critical. The head of a turkey arrow must be one that penetrates completely and easily. There are so-called turkey heads on the market that impede penetration; the theory being that they will cause more damage. I have taken the wing of a dead turkey, pinned it on a target and failed to get some of these heads to penetrate. Have you ever tried to cut in two a primary wing feather of an adult bird, with a knife? A good sharp, fairly wide two-bladed broad head is perfect. Two blades slip between large feathers as they do between the ribs of a large animal. What is even more important is keeping the arrow in the turkey once it penetrates. This is the opposite of the pass through desirable in hunting other game in order to provide a good blood trail. Any device that can be added behind the broad head that prevents it from being pulled out will help keep the arrow in the bird. Even a poorly hit bird can often be recovered as he runs into cover or tries to hide if the arrow impedes his progress or "hangs him up." As you approach the area you suspect on of these birds to be, listen carefully for the sounds of his struggle. Of these arrow retention devices I use one, formerly made by Zwickey and I understand now available through the Internet called the "Scorpio." A set of wire fingers such as are found on the "judo point" is arranged so that they fit the shaft and are marketed based on the shaft diameter. The scorpio allows the arrow to penetrate and stop only as the scorpio ceases sliding on the shaft often as it reaches the fletching. A similar looking device is marketed that fits behind the broadhead in a fixed position and this one only stops the head from penetrating any more than its own length.

Another device also use to keep the bird from escaping is the "string tracker." A friend of mine has used one very effectively. However he hunts from a pre-set blind, the environment of which is friendlier to the use of complicated add-ons. As a matter of fact he recently hit a large gobbler that, in its effort to get away, broke the string. My friend dejectedly searched for almost an hour and was about to quit when he spotted the broken end of the string. He carefully followed it and retrieved his turkey.

All of this is not important if the turkey is hit perfectly in the first place. An arrow in the head, spine or body cavity, which is only about the size of an apple, will kill a turkey on the spot. Any place else will result in a cripple or a pile of feathers. Whenever you aim at a turkey visualize the placement of these organs. I set my decoy exactly twenty paces from my seat and that is the distance for which my bow is sighted. Two things to remember when visualizing these organs is that when a turkey is puffed up his feathers are raised so that the upper half of what you see is nothing but feathers. Also, because a turkey with his fan up and covering his head provides the perfect opportunity, don't make the following mistake. Sitting in south Texas with a cameraman behind me, I heard the spit and drum of a gobbler just outside our brush blind to my left and behind. Moving nothing but my eyeballs I waited until he strutted by heading for my decoy. His fan was up all the way so as he reached the decoy my bow was already drawn and aimed at the dead center of his fan. At the shot he folded, looked surprised, and ran off. My cameraman let out a vulgar expletive. I was so sure of myself that in my haste I forgot the placement of the organs on a strutting bird. One has to aim at the anus or base of the tail to do any damage. Also keep in mind the direction the turkey is headed, as he will cock his tail so that it faces the hen. This means that his body is not always directly in line.

How about jumping the string? I don't believe a turkey will jump the string but I do know they can duck an arrow. I cut the head off a Florida turkey that tried to duck an arrow aimed for his body. At another time I had two Merriam jakes coming in through the snow. I shot at the nearest bird which ducked the arrow that ended up in the bird behind him. This incidentally was the only time I've ever had a turkey blood trail to follow. Both of the above hunts were caught on video.

The author's son Lars and a 25-lb. Vermont bird shot with his muzzle loader at 14 paces.

Any lessons learned from bowhunting can be used for muzzleloading. There is always the advantage in muzzleloading of being less erect and more mobile somewhat similar to regular shotgun shooting. But one has to take more care on being hidden, as the turkey must approach to within range. Again, either one has to set up where the turkey is within range when first seen or use a decoy. No need for a "stuffer" here, rather I prefer one or more of the very lifelike collapsible decoys like the ones made by "Carry-Lite." I have never been turned on by a vinyl blow up doll, and I don't believe any self-respecting gobbler gets too excited by the blow up vinyl decoys, not matter how easy they are to carry. The sheen of the vinyl is very flat and two-dimensional. One great addition to the equipment a muzzleloading hunter needs is the self-supporting vest such as the one made by "Bucklick Creek." This vest holds you in sitting position without a natural backrest. It also armors your butt and back from things that would stick in you when backed into nasty brush of all kinds.

Every muzzleloading shotgun has a favorite load. You must experiment with a pattern sheet and back up quarter inch plywood to find pattern and penetration of various powder and shot amounts and shot sizes that perform best in your gun. And it is also very important to experiment with various wad combinations. One good rule is to have plenty of wad over the powder to cushion and therefore cause less shot deformation and the thinnest practical card wad over the shot to prevent the wad from creating a hole in the pattern. By using the right combination of wads, powder and shot buffered with flour and contained in a paper shot cup, we are regularly killing turkeys at 25 yards and less with an unchoked 20 gauge blackpowder gun. But the difference between killing and losing badly hit birds is in research. Don't simply do what another hunter suggests because there are more variations in guns, barrels and chokes than you realize. Consider all the research and development done by the major manufacturers of shot shells in order to build the perfect turkey cartridge. You are merely doing the same every time you load a muzzleloader. Of course if the bird is close enough there is only the need for a decent aim. There are ways to insure this without a decoy no matter with what you are hunting. One, set up within range of a bend in a road, trail or opening in the brush that a turkey must pass before coming into sight on its way to you. Two, set up just over the top of a knoll, ridge or bank where the turkey must come into sight within range. There is a great temptation to set up where the turkey can be observed as he moves all the way to your position. Third, set up in a place that through scouting you have determined that a turkey feels safe passing. In Vermont many gobblers have been shot as they traveled through barways in fences and walls. Lastly and a favorite of mine, when the opportunity presents itself call in a real hen, she will then do all the calling and decoying for you.

One early morning this spring, gobblers answered each other at either end of a Vermont ridge I was sitting under. This continued until they left the roost and then all went quiet. I had a long silent wait. Then I heard a far off hen who I immediately imitated as best I could. Each time she called I answered. It didn't take long for her to arrive, and when I went silent and she couldn't find me she went bananas. The hen stood on a bank in front of me and made the darndest racket. Soon there were gobbles in all directions. Five jakes with a long beard in tow came in from my right and there was more gobbling to my left. The hen now having not found me but having attracted so much attention decided to wander off. I called and the mature bird strutted just out of range. The five jakes circled me sometimes a mere ten yards away, but I was hoping for a shot at the big boy. Eventually he worked off to my right and things had scarcely calmed down when another mature bird came into my sight at my left. He strutted to the place on the bank that the hen had done her calling and in almost an hour of strutting and gobbling, he never gave me the opportunity to move. I was tempted several times to chance a shot but it was not to be. With my old 870 Remington in my hand at least one gobbler would have ended up in the freezer but I would have missed all the fun.

Finally, a year ago last spring I had patterned the habits of a gobbler that roosted above some ledges and eventually worked his way down an old skid-road. One morning I slipped in early and sunk into the hole left by an uprooted birch. Only my head and shoulders were above ground level and my back was against the upturned roots. What a hide! I answered him on the roost with a few soft clucks and then put my call down and waited, gun up and I concentrated on the skid-road where it came into sight about twenty yards away. Quite awhile had passed since I heard his last gobble and I was sure he was on his way. Suddenly I was showered with dirt from the roots overhead and jumped in surprise. With that a gobbler tumbled into some briars a few feet to my left. I threw up my gun and fired point blank and of course missed completely. He flew from there up into a tree where he sat trying to figure out what had just happened. As I tried to figure out the same, I realized that he had come down a different way and had hopped up on the fallen birch, walked it, then jumped to the roots, from where he had expected to see the hen he had previously heard, and in the process knocked the dirt on my head. Now that is just too "uptight."

Appendix

DOs AND DON'Ts

Do: Find out all you can about turkeys and turkey hunting before you try it.

Don't: Wait for the season to start to locate turkeys to hunt.

Do: Practice your calling until you have confidence in your abilities.

Don't: Try out your calling on turkeys you plan to hunt later during the season.

Do: Scout and learn turkey patterns of movement before opening day.

Don't: Go on private land without permission.

Do: Look for gobblers in places where you have found them before.

Do: "Roost" turkeys the night before the hunt.

Do: Use locator type calls to get a response from the gobbler when scouting and roosting.

Don't: Depend on turkeys answering gobbling from their roosts, even if you already know they are there.

Do: Pattern your gun before the season.

Don't: Try calling a bird during the season without being prepared to set-up on him.

Do: Use complete camouflage, including hands and face.

Do: Pick a set up that breaks your entire outline and blends with your camouflage.

Don't: Set-up where there is a natural barrier that the turkey will not come through.

Don't: Set-up where a turkey must approach into a low bright sun.

Don't: Set-up where a low bright sun shines in your eyes or on your equipment.

Do: Pick a spot if possible where there is something the arriving turkey must pass behind so you can get your gun up without being seen.

Don't: Place yourself in a position where you can't swing your gun 90 degrees left or right of the approaching turkey.

Do: Be patient and don't move when working a turkey.

Don't: Make loud yelps at a roosting turkey.

Don't: Make loud yelps at a gobbler that is close to you.

Don't: Make loud yelps late in the season.

Don't: Continue calling to a roosting bird once he indicates he has heard you.

Do: Remember the different stages of spring behavior and hunt accordingly.

Don't: Move on your turkey until you find out what he does when you stop calling.

Do: Use clucks and soft calls in the late season.

Don't: Gobble unless your are challenging a dominant bird.

Do: Use your cackle when hunting jakes.

Don't: Stop calling if you make a mistake.

Don't: Quit hunting early. Late morning when hens may have left a gobbler is often the best.

Do: Be aware of other turkeys around that might give you away when you move to shoot.

Don't: Shoot at a bird out of range.

Do: Change your focus and look for obstructions between you and the turkey you are about to shoot.

Don't: Try to "out draw" a turkey. A moving turkey that has seen you is nearly impossible to kill with a clean head shot.

Don't: Shoot until your gun is properly cheeked and sighted.

Do: Get to your turkey as fast as possible and immobilize him after the shot.

Don't: Pick up a struggling turkey.

Do: Be sure of your target.

Don't: Stalk turkeys.

Do: Make them come to you.

Do: Set-up so you are protected from gunfire from the rear.

Don't: Wear or carry reds, whites, and blues.

Don't: Call to another hunter with your turkey calls.

Don't: Gobble unless you feel it is safe and necessary.

Don't: Wave at an approaching hunter or move until you are sure that he has recognized you as a man.

Don't: Move through the woods calling, particularly in the fall.

Do: Carry your dead bird by the head or in a bag.

Do: Educate new turkey hunters on the safe and ethical ways to hunt the grandest of game birds.

INDEX